Corporate-NGO Partnership in Asia Pacific

Corporate-NGO Partnership in Asia Pacific

coedited by
Tadashi Yamamoto
and
Kim Gould Ashizawa

JCIE

Tokyo • Japan Center for International Exchange • *New York*

Copyright 1999 © Japan Center for International Exchange
All rights reserved.

Copyediting by Pamela J. Noda.
Cover and typographic design by Becky Davis, EDS Inc.,
Editorial & Design Services. Typesetting and production by EDS Inc.
Cover photograph © 1997 Joe Ginsberg/PhotoDisc, Inc.

Printed in Japan.
ISBN 4-88907-038-9

Distributed worldwide outside Japan by Brookings Institution Press,
1775 Massachusetts Avenue, N.W., Washington, D.C. 20036-2188 U.S.A.

Japan Center for International Exchange
9-17 Minami Azabu 4-chome, Minato-ku, Tokyo 106-0047 Japan

URL: http://www.jcie.or.jp

Japan Center for International Exchange, Inc. (JCIE/USA)
1251 Avenue of the Americas, New York, N.Y. 10020 U.S.A.

Contents

Foreword

THE Japan Center for International Exchange (JCIE) launched the Corporate-NGO Partnership Project in the summer of 1997. The project was intended to be a follow-up to, and an extension of, two clusters of civil society–related activities in which JCIE has been involved over the past several years, working with such like-minded organizations as the Asia Pacific Philanthropy Consortium (APPC), the Council on Foundations in the United States, and Keidanren (Japan Federation of Economic Organizations). One cluster of projects was designed to assess the evolution of civil society organizations in Asia Pacific, with an emphasis on NGOs. The other cluster of projects consisted of more recent efforts to study the developing patterns of foreign and indigenous corporations' philanthropic activities in Asia Pacific. A noticeable trend toward convergence between these two clusters of activities was observed in the mid-1990s, as corporations showed growing interest in working with the emerging civil society.

The Corporate-NGO Partnership Project was initiated in the belief that case studies examining the diverse patterns of corporate-NGO partnership in Asia Pacific would enable the development of a better understanding of the complex dynamics of interaction between organizations from these two sectors, and would produce at least tentative criteria for successful partnership in the Asian context. While an increasing amount of literature on corporate social responsibility and corporate community involvement in Asia Pacific has been published, including a previous JCIE

7

study titled *Emerging Civil Society in the Asia Pacific Community*, there has been little in-depth analysis of the evolving pattern of corporate-NGO partnership in the region. It was therefore hoped that this case study project and its dissemination efforts would further enhance the examination of requirements for bringing about effective corporate-NGO partnership.

This publication represents an important component of the efforts to disseminate the major findings on and future agenda of corporate-NGO partnership. However, dissemination of the results of the case study project actually began with a conference organized by JCIE in June 1999, which was cosponsored by APPC and Keidanren, as well as two Keidanren affiliates, the Council for Better Corporate Citizenship and the One Percent Club. The meeting focused on the findings of the case studies and most of the researchers involved in the project participated. The discussions at the Tokyo Conference on Corporate-NGO Partnership in Asia Pacific confirmed our assumption that the case studies project would stimulate active interaction among people working in corporations and NGOs, as well as those in other diverse sectors. Many new insights into this relatively new subject were generated through those discussions, and they have been reflected in the overview in chapter 1 of this publication.

The launch of the case study project was very much encouraged by a request for a proposal extended by the Hitachi Foundation in the United States, which hoped to "leverage successful results" produced by projects it had supported in the past, including the aforementioned volume *Emerging Civil Society*. JCIE wishes to express its deep gratitude to the Hitachi Foundation for its generous support, which has made this project possible. I also wish to thank APPC and Keidanren for their support of the Tokyo conference, which represented the final phase of the project.

The Corporate-NGO Partnership Project was truly a collaborative effort involving many partners. Researchers from JCIE and numerous civil society leaders from Asian countries worked closely together to produce the case studies through interviews, field trips, and workshops. I was inspired by their commitment and friendship, and learned a great deal from them throughout the project. I am particularly grateful to the efforts of Hideko Katsumata and Mio Kawashima of JCIE, who coordinated the complex process of the case studies. I am most grateful for the dedicated work of Kim Gould Ashizawa, who joined the project in its final phase as the coeditor of this publication, providing substantial editorial assistance to the case study writers—for many of whom English is not their mother tongue—and working closely with me to finalize all of the manuscripts. I also wish to thank Pamela J. Noda and the editorial staff of JCIE for their support.

TADASHI YAMAMOTO
President
Japan Center for International Exchange

Corporate-NGO Partnership in Asia Pacific

1 Corporate-NGO Partnership: Learning from Case Studies

Tadashi Yamamoto

THERE was an air of excitement in the room as some 80 corporate managers and leaders from civil society organizations gathered in Tokyo on June 7–8, 1999. These individuals, primarily from countries in Asia Pacific, had come together to discuss the outcome of case studies undertaken by the Japan Center for International Exchange (JCIE) on partnership in Asia Pacific between corporations and nongovernmental organizations (NGOs). The venue of the conference was Keidanren (Japan Federation of Economic Organizations), a building that was once a favorite target of NGO demonstrations, picketed by those criticizing corporate practices that caused environmental degradation and other serious social problems. To have a discussion on corporate-NGO partnership in this citadel of Japan's corporate world was in itself a cause for considerable excitement.

As the discussion unfolded at the conference, it became evident that corporations in many countries in Asia Pacific are seriously seeking a new pattern for their philanthropic activities and have begun to increase their engagement in communities by working in close cooperation with NGOs. The case studies indicated that a growing number of NGOs in Asia are actively pursuing partnerships with corporations as they attempt to meet heightened expectations for the nonprofit sector to play a larger role, particularly in the wake of the recent financial crisis that has devastated the lives of people in the region.

The enthusiasm generated at the Tokyo conference as the participants discussed the cases of successful partnership arrangements seemed to reflect the hopes and aspirations of leaders in both the corporate community and civil society that these partnerships can further enhance the emergence of civil society in the region, and at the same time provide added impetus for corporate philanthropic activities to evolve toward new and effective patterns of community involvement.

BACKGROUND OF THE CORPORATE-NGO PARTNERSHIP PROJECT

EMERGENCE OF AND CHALLENGES TO CIVIL SOCIETY IN ASIA PACIFIC

A general picture of the impressive growth of civil society in the region has been drawn by several recent studies, including a volume edited by this author, titled *Emerging Civil Society in the Asia Pacific Community,* which was published in 1995 on the basis of a survey project covering 15 countries in Asia Pacific.[1] One of the most notable trends in the development of civil society in the region has been the distinct growth of indigenous NGOs. In addition to an expansion in the size of the sector, there has clearly been an evolution in the scope and nature of NGO activities. NGOs have begun to transform themselves from traditional organizations that provide charitable contributions and services to the poor into organizations that directly involve themselves in addressing issues in developing countries, such as rural development, poverty alleviation, nutrition and health, reproductive biology, and education, and global issues such as environmental preservation, human rights, refugees, and the population crisis. Moreover, these NGOs in Asian countries have begun to establish networks among themselves, which is another new phenomenon in the region.

On the other hand, studies of newly developing Asian countries, as well as of advanced countries such as Japan, draw particular attention to the considerable constraints faced by NGOs. Specifically, many country reports indicate the dire need for most indigenous NGOs to secure a more stable funding base to enable them to function professionally and effectively. In addition, the challenges facing NGOs in Asia in securing autonomy from their respective governments makes heavy reliance on

1. Tadashi Yamamoto, ed., *Emerging Civil Society in the Asia Pacific Community* (Singapore: Institute of Southeast Asian Studies and Japan Center for International Exchange), 1995.

government funding undesirable. Overall, these recent studies and debates over civil society development in Asia clearly indicate a mismatch between the demand side and the supply side of civil society—namely, between NGOs and their funding sources.

EVOLUTION OF CORPORATE PHILANTHROPHY IN ASIA PACIFIC

Several projects in recent years have attempted to address this issue of supply and demand.[2] These projects have been premised upon the understanding that the recent rapid economic development in many Asian countries, which is often characterized as "corporate-driven," has given rise to greater indigenous corporate community involvement and support for NGOs. The increasing number of companies from North America, Europe, and Japan entering the Asian market has also resulted in a significant growth in philanthropic involvement on the part of these corporations in their host countries. Consequently, these studies found that corporate philanthropy, though still limited in scale and scope, is rapidly growing and clearly has the potential to provide a significant financial base for the emerging civil society in the Asia Pacific region.

Indeed, corporations appear to have started adding a new dimension to their philanthropic activities by developing partnerships with emerging Asian NGOs rather than merely continuing the traditional pattern of charitable giving. This seems to be a reflection of the growing recognition in Asian societies of NGOs as effective actors in dealing with diverse development issues, as well as a reflection of corporate strategies that are emphasizing closer community involvement through work with NGOs. There also seems to be a growing recognition by corporations that partnership with NGOs is instrumental in gaining broad public participation in, and support for, philanthropic activities.

This new direction in corporate philanthropy in Asia Pacific, however, requires a more sophisticated approach on the part of corporations in defining priority areas, identifying NGO partners, and using the expertise of intermediary organizations. At the same time, the emerging pattern of

2. These projects have included a conference held in September 1995, in Hong Kong, on the theme of "Corporate Citizenship in Asia Pacific," organized by the Council on Foundations together with members of the Asia Pacific Philanthropy Consortium (APPC), which had been formed in 1994; a conference organized by APPC in Bangkok in January 1998, on the theme of "Supporting the Nonprofit Sector in Asia"; and a 1996 Keidanren mission to the United States to study corporate-NGO partnership experiences.

partnership with corporations presents NGOs with new challenges as well. They need to motivate and sustain corporate partners while demonstrating their own expertise, and they need to maintain their basic characteristic as autonomous and innovative actors in society without becoming corporate subsidiaries.

CASE STUDIES AS A PROCESS
OF REGIONAL CORPORATE-NGO PARTNERSHIP

The Corporate-NGO Partnership Project comprised a series of case studies and meetings that aimed at examining the diverse patterns of corporate-NGO partnership in Asia Pacific. While there has been an increasing amount of literature that deals with general topics of corporate social responsibility and corporate community involvement in Asia Pacific, there has been little in-depth analysis of the evolving pattern of corporate-NGO partnership in the region. It was therefore hoped that this case study project would further stimulate exploration by corporate and NGO leaders to strengthen their cooperative relationships.

In fact, the process of implementing the case studies proved to be a joint effort between individuals representing the business and nonprofit sectors from many countries in Asia Pacific, and thus the project itself represents a corporate-NGO partnership on a broad regional basis. The intensity of the process, as well as the active interaction among participants from diverse professional backgrounds at the Tokyo conference, reinforced an underlying assumption of this project that corporate and NGO leaders are aggressively seeking the means to implement effective corporate-NGO partnership.

The first phase of the project was the selection of the cases to be studied, which was done through a literature survey and through informal consultations with key members of the Asia Pacific Philanthropy Consortium and field staff of such international foundations as the Ford Foundation and the Asia Foundation. Cases were selected to ensure a diverse range of corporations in terms of national origin, business sector, and NGO partners. It was believed that such a selection would provide a basis for cross-analysis of the various partnership arrangements of external and indigenous corporations and NGOs in various fields. Attention was given to the functions and specific activities of intermediary organizations that facilitated partnership arrangements.

The second phase of the project was the recruitment of researchers and writers for the selected cases, followed by initial consultations, most of which took place through face-to-face meetings. The project director and JCIE staff were assigned to cases involving American and Japanese corporations, and indigenous writers were asked to cover cases in China, Indonesia, the Philippines, and Thailand. The two cases in Vietnam were genuine collaborative efforts by a team of Japanese and Vietnamese researchers.

The third phase of the project entailed the actual research activities, including field visits. The project director visited the headquarters of the American and British corporations included in the case studies, traveling to New York, San Francisco, and London for personal interviews. The director and JCIE staff also visited the researchers in Asia for intense consultations. A workshop, hosted by the Japan Foundation Bangkok office, was held in August 1998, bringing together several researchers and JCIE research staff to compare notes on the progress of the research. Another workshop was held in November 1998, in Washington, D.C., with the participation of officers from the Hitachi Foundation, JCIE staff, one case writer from the Philippines, and several resource persons, to compare notes on the preliminary findings of the project.

In the fourth phase of the project, the research papers were summarized by Kim Gould Ashizawa, coeditor of the project, for the final conference and for this publication. The full text of the original case studies will also be made available on the JCIE Web site.[3]

The Tokyo Conference on Corporate-NGO Partnership in Asia Pacific was the final phase of the project, bringing together representatives of the corporations and NGOs that were taken up in the case studies. In addition, representatives from a number of other corporations offered their perspectives based on their own experiences with corporate-NGO partnerships. These corporations included Yuhan-Kimberly of South Korea, PT Rio Tinto of Indonesia, Royal and Sun Alliance Insurance Group of the United Kingdom, Sony Corporation, Nissan Motors, Asahi Brewery, and Fuji-Xerox. Although corporate-NGO partnership still has a relatively brief history in the region, there was a clear manifestation of willingness among these corporate and NGO leaders to share their experiences with others in order to foster more productive working relationships.

The case studies and the subsequent discussions in Tokyo elicited a number of fresh insights into this relatively new subject, and have pointed to issues that will have to be addressed in the coming years. This volume

3. The URL for JCIE's Web site is < http://www.jcie.or.jp >.

is designed to share with interested individuals in business, civil society, government, politics, media, and other sectors the major findings on and future agenda of corporate-NGO partnership.

THE EVOLVING CONTEXT FOR CORPORATE-NGO PARTNERSHIP

IMPACT ON CIVIL SOCIETY

When the Corporate-NGO Partnership Project was first conceived, most nations in Asia were still enjoying the consequences of the phenomenal economic growth often referred to as the "East Asian miracle." It is clear that the remarkable economic development of the past decade or two contributed greatly, and in diverse ways, to the growth of civil society in Asia. In one sense, the emergence of a middle class in these countries was critical to the development of private nonprofit organizations. Many public-spirited development NGOs in Asian countries, established during the latter part of the 1980s and the early part of the 1990s, were organizations formed primarily by individuals from the middle class. These individuals were able to reflect on and articulate a growing concern for the environment, human rights, and democratization that was emerging most visibly within that social stratum. It can also be argued, however, that the negative consequences of rapid economic development in the region have contributed equally to the rise of civil society in Asia. NGOs claim that Asian governments have not been able to bring about equitable economic development, and that it is therefore the responsibility of the nongovernmental sector to come up with alternative policies that can offer a more equitable distribution of the benefits of economic growth.

The technological advances made during the past decades have also affected civil society. Many NGOs consider their role to be that of reflecting concerns about the social and material condition of economically and socially disadvantaged people and bringing those concerns to the national agenda. Their activities have been substantially enhanced and empowered by the availability of highly advanced communications technology, which has enabled them to share information among themselves instantaneously and to forge joint strategies in promoting their causes.

The era of rapid economic growth in Asia came to an abrupt end in July 1997. The financial crisis that has beset many Asian countries since that time has had a major impact on NGOs in Asia, presenting them with greater challenges than ever before. The expectations placed upon civil society have grown as economic conditions have worsened. The human impact of the crisis has become evident in many areas: falling real incomes and a rising incidence of poverty; increasing levels of unemployment; growing migration flows; emerging food shortages and malnutrition; declining public health; falling rates of participation in education; and an increasing incidence of crime. In the face of this crisis, many Asian governments have been pressed to downsize drastically and, concomitantly, to reduce their budget allocation for dealing with the human and social impact of the crisis. Under such circumstances, civil society is expected to play a greater role in the creation of adequate social safety nets to protect the unemployed, the poor, and the marginalized in society. In particular, one of the most important contributions that civil society is making in the wake of the crisis is to redirect the development strategies of many governments away from a fixation on growth rates and toward a more holistic conception of human development.

Moreover, the financial crisis has broadened the debate over the role of civil society organizations in these Asian countries. There has been growing public acceptance of the idea that civil society organizations are forces of sociopolitical and economic reform that can contribute to improvements in the governance of society. The deficiency of governance in many of these countries has come to the fore as the crisis, to a great extent, has been attributed to the absence of transparency and accountability in Asian governments. It was reported at the Tokyo conference, for example, that among all the nonprofit organizations in South Korea, citizen advocacy groups in particular have gained visibility and momentum since the financial crisis because the economic debacle has been associated with the systemic failure of the old system of governance.

From another perspective, the challenges faced by civil society organizations in Asia have been exacerbated as they have faced growing demands to help alleviate social problems, including increased government reliance on them to help deal with the dire social problems facing the region. There is concern among NGO leaders that such sudden expectations from governments, when accompanied by funding, can undermine the autonomous nature of NGOs. For example, the Japanese government recently proposed to provide a large amount of funding to increase employment opportunities in nonprofit organizations as a way of addressing the country's current unemployment situation. This idea has been challenged by many NGO leaders in Japan (some of whom participated in the Tokyo conference), who view the proposal as being based on an assumption that NGOs are government subsidiaries that can be called upon conveniently to alleviate serious social problems and then be deserted once the immediate problem has been solved. An Indonesian participant reported that this sudden rise in expectations regarding the role that NGOs can play is straining the absorptive capacity of these fragile organizations, and may also undermine the steady progress that was being made toward institution building. In addition, as the influence of civil society and expectations for its contributions have grown, questions have arisen about the legitimacy and accountability of NGOs, and about their tendency to focus on single issues rather than the broader public interest.

IMPACT ON CORPORATE PHILANTHROPY

When Asian countries were going through periods of phenomenal economic gains, a growing number of corporations, both indigenous and foreign, were increasing their support for efforts to address social needs. As the summary report of a 1995 Hong Kong conference on "Corporate Citizenship in Asia Pacific" indicated, "As corporations endeavor to grow and sustain new markets around the world, they are frequently confronted with social, legal and economic conditions that affect the production and sale of their products and services." The result, the report concludes, is often "an appreciation for the relationship between corporate self-interest and the health of communities."[4]

As corporations expanded their role as engines of economic growth in Asia Pacific countries, their impact on society became stronger. A growing trend emerged whereby corporations began to depart from traditional patterns of charitable giving for the poor and the needy to actively engage themselves in dealing with social problems. In doing so, corporations started to regard NGOs as useful partners in effectively responding to the needs of their stakeholders.

A new generation of managers and owners has also played a role in transforming the way that corporations interact with the broader society. Younger executives hold different views from their predecessors on the roles and responsibilities of their companies. Accordingly, many companies have come to consider corporate responsibility to be an essential component of their overall business strategy and not simply a public

4. Lori A. Vacek, "Corporate Citizenship in Asia Pacific—A Conference Report," prepared for the Conference on Corporate Citizenship in Asia Pacific (Hong Kong, September 19–22), 1995, p. 3.

relations activity. Corporations operating in Asia have come to recognize that their long-term success is closely related to the health and stability of the societies in which they operate.

Despite these positive trends, the Asian financial crisis has dealt a devastating blow to many indigenous and global corporations operating in the region, resulting in the curtailment of some philanthropic activities, as witnessed in several cases covered in this project. At the same time, however, these corporations have also come under pressure to support NGOs that have been mobilized to provide relief to those hit hard by the crisis.

Corporations have also found themselves under fire recently for their arcane pattern of corporate governance, such as the absence of transparency and accountability, which is considered to have been one of the causes of the economic debacle in the region. Accordingly, corporations—both indigenous and foreign—are increasingly expected to contribute to the development of viable communities and sustainable markets and to the achievement of a more effective system of governance in cooperation with the public and nongovernmental sectors. Also, as corporations are more deeply involved than ever before in domestic and international politics, they are more likely to be held accountable by governments and the public for the economic consequences of their activities. Thus, they have come under pressure to participate more actively in addressing social agendas. In discharging such new responsibilities, many corporations have found that partnerships with civil society organizations, which often represent certain values and concerns of the community, are an effective approach.

GROWING IMPORTANCE OF
CROSS-SECTORAL PARTNERSHIPS IN ASIA

Most countries in Asia that achieved the "East Asian miracle" in the 1980s and early 1990s had a system of governance well suited to pursue the single purpose of rapid economic growth. Governments were considered to be the sole arbiter of public goods during that period, and both corporations and nonprofit organizations were put under their control or were subject to their guidance. These traditional systems of governance, which worked well for many years in countries such as Japan and South Korea, have been shaken not only by the financial crisis but by broader forces of globalization that have created complex social issues and have required fundamental domestic adjustments. As a result, it has become quite obvious that many of the region's governments can no longer cope with the rapidly growing social needs, and this has created a widening space for new actors from the NGO and corporate sectors.

In the case of Japan, it took a tragic earthquake to serve as a galvanizing event, bringing the role of civil society to the attention of leaders in government, politics, and business, and attracting the focus of the mass media. Civil society had already begun to deal with the country's pluralistic needs over the past decade or so, but the impressive on-site relief work of more than 1.3 million volunteers and NGOs following the Great Hanshin-Awaji Earthquake of 1995 touched off a movement—joined by NGO leaders, business leaders, national legislators, and the media—that led to the passage of landmark legislation in March 1998 which will facilitate the establishment of civil society organizations and give them greater autonomy from the government bureaucracy.

In many Asian countries, governments have started to reach out to NGOs, viewing them as valuable partners that can offer unique expertise, perspectives, and resources. The case study of the Panmai Group, for example, points out that Thailand's Eighth National Economic and Social Development Plan (1997–2001) emphasizes the concept of multiparty participation in development efforts, which incorporates the public sector, the private business sector, NGOs, the mass media, academic institutions, and private citizens. In the case of the Cebu Hillyland Development Program in the Philippines, a local government official actually served as the initiator and intermediary in the creation of a partnership. It was the mayor of Cebu City who approached the Philippine Business for Social Progress for its assistance in tapping the resources of the business community to work with farmers, and who also convinced the farmers of the sincerity of the companies in their willingness to build a partnership.

The evolving environment in Asia is particularly conducive to cross-sectoral partnerships in that the problems facing society are increasingly complex and interconnected. Finding solutions will require multiple sources of talent, resources, and expertise, drawing on attributes found within all sectors of society. When based on the respective strengths of those involved, these partnerships can extend the benefits of each partner's resources, dignify and empower all parties involved, and amplify the impact of their efforts.[5] Business, in particular, is regarded as a valuable partner, offering unique contributions to the resolution of social problems,

5. Colin Campbell, "Forging Partnerships among Diverse Interests," *CAF Focus* (newsletter of the Charities Aid Foundation), Paper No. 1 (May 1998), p. 4.

including research and development expertise, distribution services, outreach, and marketing support, as well as traditional giving and community involvement assistance.

The forces of democratization that have taken root in many Asian countries, although still constrained by authoritarian regimes in some cases, have substantially reduced the ideological conflicts between government and business on the one hand, and NGOs on the other, that has made collaboration among these sectors difficult in the past. While government bureaucrats in Asian countries still tend to regard NGOs as their convenient subsidiaries, there seems to be a growing recognition among them that NGOs are effective precisely because of their independence from the government. Conversely, increasing numbers of NGOs are becoming more self-confident and mature, and are allowing themselves to forge partnerships with government and business. Among leaders throughout these societies, the financial crisis in Asia has brought about much greater recognition than ever before of the need for productive partnerships among diverse sectors in order to meet new challenges, address multiple and deepening social needs, and undertake the formidable task of structural reforms to bring about a more effective and equitable system of governance.

WHY PARTNERSHIP?—CORPORATE PERSPECTIVES

NGOS AS FACILITATORS
OF CORPORATE COMMUNITY INVOLVEMENT

All of the cases taken up in the Corporate-NGO Partnership Project demonstrate the increasing attention that corporations are giving to the health of the communities in which they operate. Many participants in the Tokyo conference underscored the fact that a growing number of corporations have changed the emphasis of their philanthropic activities from charitable giving to community involvement, thus creating a conducive environment for partnership with NGOs and other sectors working in the same communities.

The case study on China found this type of new trend emerging among corporations in that country, although it is still a relatively recent phenomenon. An increasing number of private enterprises are beginning to seek more than publicity from their community activities. Looking instead for ways to fulfill their social responsibility, they have begun contributing to such causes as the environment, poverty alleviation, education, and welfare. Bankers Trust is an example of a company that has shifted its emphasis to the community. Roughly a decade ago, Bankers Trust decided to maximize the benefits to both the community and the firm itself by tightening the focus of its corporate philanthropy programs. As a result, the company chose to concentrate on working with local NGOs in the belief that it should rely on and foster the development of capable NGOs as agents for change in the communities in which the bank operates. An officer in charge of social contribution activities for Nissan Motors reported at the Tokyo conference that it was also about ten years ago that her company and many other Japanese companies began getting directly involved in addressing social issues, which they found necessitated that they work with NGOs.

A number of corporations have turned their attention to environmental issues as an area that concerns them both as an economic entity and on an individual basis. Obviously, the environment represents an area of common concern for many communities, as well as an area in which a large number of NGOs are active, and it is therefore a fertile field for partnerships. Indonesia's leading producer of bottled water, PT Aqua Golden Mississippi, is a case in point, as it responded to criticism from local NGOs by forming a partnership project for PET bottle recycling. The Cebu Hillyland partnership project in the Philippines is similarly a case where corporations understood that the preservation of upland watershed areas through community development and reforestation was in their own best interest, because the water supply was a critical resource for them, as well as in the interest of the local communities.

These and other illustrations found in the cases presented in this volume clearly demonstrate that an increasing number of corporations are finding it essential to forge partnerships with NGOs that have access to community residents, can readily identify community needs, and are equipped with professional expertise to meet such needs. In their attempt to serve the communities more effectively, some corporate managers at the conference noted that they have found the "innovativeness" of NGOs in addressing social issues to be most useful.

PROFESSIONAL EXPERTISE OF NGOS RESPONDS TO COMMUNITY NEEDS

One unique advantage that NGOs offer their corporate partners is professional expertise to respond to the needs of the communities in which corporations are or wish to be active. When British Petroleum decided to engage in community involvement activities in Vietnam, it connected with Save the Children to launch the Poverty Alleviation and Nutrition Program, relying fully on the competence and experience of this international NGO. British Petroleum also formed a partnership with Fauna and Flora International, another international NGO, to undertake the Cuc Phuong National Park Conservation Project. It should be noted that in both cases, the professional expertise of these NGOs included their capacity to work with community organizations and villages. Philippine Business for Social Progress used its expertise in development and environmental protection to bring about an initial partnership between business and government; it then incorporated community organizations as well in the Cebu Hillyland Development Program.

NGOs' professional expertise has been called upon in several cases when corporations wished to localize their philanthropic and community involvement activities. Bankers Trust entered into a partnership with Philippine Business for Social Progress and the Ayala Foundation to carry out the Barangay Improvement Project in Manila, believing that working with local NGOs who are familiar with local needs, language, society, and culture is critical for the success of any international project in which Bankers Trust is involved. Levi Strauss & Co. started an innovative community involvement project in Japan in 1997, through a donor advised fund given to JCIE, which acts as an intermediary, distributing the funds to NGOs in Japan in accordance with general guidelines set by Levi Strauss & Co. This mechanism has enabled the company to leverage JCIE's in-country expertise and networks.

NGOS AS A MEANS OF IMPLEMENTING BUSINESS STRATEGY

Barnett Baron, co-chair of the Asia Pacific Philanthropy Consortium and executive vice president of the Asia Foundation, pointed out in his opening remarks at the Tokyo conference that corporations tend not to see themselves as replacing philanthropic foundations or governments as sources of financial support for NGOs. He stated that "more and more corporations have come to view corporate citizenship in cooperation with NGOs as part of a business strategy that must respond to their core business interests and their multiple constituencies." The case studies and discussion at the Tokyo conference emphasized the fact that corporations are finding that working with local NGOs, which respond to the needs of stakeholders in the communities, is of benefit to themselves.

The practical benefits for corporations can be recognized at several different levels. One particular quality that corporations are able to make use of is the reputation and acceptance of certain NGOs in the communities. It was pointed out by some participants at the Tokyo conference that in the increasingly competitive worldwide business environment, having a technological edge does not count as much as it used to. Image and reputation are therefore providing corporations with a decisive edge over their competitors. It was also pointed out that NGOs have been very critical of companies that engage in partnership arrangements simply for the sake of projecting an image, or for public relations purposes. Aurora "Rory" Tolentino, co-chair of the Asia Pacific Philanthropy Consortium and executive director of the Ayala Foundation, emphasized in the closing comments of the Tokyo conference that companies should recognize that "image building without any substance to it will show through, and people will know it."

On another level, corporations are finding that working with NGOs can enable them to have a better understanding of their market and of customer needs. NGOs can also facilitate a corporation's approach to local markets. The Bankers Trust case, for example, reports that NGO partnerships have enabled Bankers Trust representatives to network with other leaders, government officials, and prospective clients outside of the usual business forums. Yasuda Fire and Marine Insurance Co. (Yasuda Kasai) encourages its local branch managers to become members of NGOs in the area, and this community-friendly approach has convinced many local sales agencies to become Yasuda Kasai agencies. And Toyota Motor Corporation, as part of its work with NGO partners, tries to mobilize its car dealers across Japan to reach out effectively to communities.

NGO PARTNERSHIP FOR THE IMPROVEMENT OF CORPORATE GOVERNANCE

Though a pragmatic, bottom-line approach may be gaining strength among corporations that tend to regard partnership with NGOs as a part of business strategy, many corporate participants maintained that partnership with NGOs is an important element in establishing their own identity in society and improving their corporate governance. In his keynote speech at the Tokyo conference, Yotaro Kobayashi, chairman of Fuji-Xerox Corporation and chairman of the Japan Association of Corporate Executives (Keizai Doyukai), noted that profit making is the essential means by which his company tries to achieve its founding objectives, but it is by no means the ultimate objective. Corporations are under pressure from two sides: on the one hand, there is pressure to be more productive and profitable, while on the other hand, there is pressure from the stakeholders to be more viable from a broader societal perspective. Kobayashi emphasized that the balancing of these requirements is part of the critical agenda that a new system of corporate governance should address, and that partnership with NGOs seems to be an appropriate means to strike this balance.

Several corporations analyzed in the case studies and in cases presented at the Tokyo conference underscored Kobayashi's view, having expressed their clear commitment to working with NGOs as part of their corporate philosophies. As one participant observed, the fact that a company chooses to form a partnership with an NGO entails a higher degree of commitment than unilateral forms of community involvement, and has a stronger impact on the corporation itself as well. Partnership with Dana Mitra Lingkungan, an environmental NGO in Indonesia, influenced PT Aqua Golden Mississippi, the producer of bottled water, to become a more environmentally concerned company. An increasing number of corporations are seconding their employees to NGO partners, which influences the company's and employees' attitudes toward communities and by extension influences the environment within the company. As Kobayashi pointed out, such programs have a profound influence on both corporate culture and corporate governance.

WHY PARTNERSHIP?—NGO PERSPECTIVES

The increasing attention being given by NGOs to partnership with corporations is based, in the first instance, on an interest in capital mobilization either in the form of cash or gifts-in-kind. None of the cases studied in the Corporate-NGO Partnership Project could have gotten off the ground without corporate funding. Such corporate support has become important for NGOs in part because of the dwindling availability of public funding that has resulted from the budget constraints facing many governments. It should be noted, however, that NGOs also seek corporate financial contributions for strategic reasons, since having multiple sources of funding helps them to avoid the government control that can result from exclusive reliance on public funding. One major problem for NGOs in seeking corporate funding, however, is that they normally do not have direct contact with potential corporate contributors. The problem is even more daunting for small NGOs, and as will be discussed in greater detail subsequently, the use of intermediary organizations is essential for them in seeking corporate contributions.

Second, the business sector is regarded as a valuable partner from the NGO perspective because it can offer unique contributions to the resolution of social problems, including research and development expertise, distribution services, outreach, and marketing support. Marketing skills, for example, are important for NGOs since many of them provide services to citizens or earn income from their products and services. The case study on Indonesia describes NGOs becoming involved in the business of recycling PET bottles, while the case study on the women weavers of the Panmai Group Partnership tells how this group began to sell gasoline in addition to clothing as a way of earning funds for themselves and their community. An increasing number of NGOs are becoming business-like, and partnership with corporations is a powerful instrument for these NGOs to develop a self-sustaining pattern of activities.

NGOs badly need certain management skills, such as financial management, information technology, and strategic planning, which are essential to building a stronger institutional infrastructure. Strategic partnership with corporations provides NGOs with access to skills and training that they would otherwise not be able to afford. Such transfers of valuable human resources from corporations to NGOs has become even more effective through corporate volunteer activities and secondment of corporate staff—activities which have been increasing significantly in Asian countries in recent years. Bankers Trust's local staff in the Philippines helped villagers with business plans and provided technical assistance that allowed local NGOs to build new roads and other infrastructure on their own.

Third, corporations bring to the partnership a sense of accountability and a hard-nosed, result-oriented attitude that is often lacking in their NGO counterparts. Some NGO representatives at the Tokyo conference pointed out that NGOs have to develop harder measures of impact and outputs, and not concentrate only on the process. The corporate focus on cost efficiency, for example, is something that NGOs can learn through partnership with businesses.

Fourth, corporations can support their NGO partners by utilizing their political influence. The Cebu Hillyland Development partnership case illustrates strong support from corporate partners for their NGO counterparts in fighting a land development project that was considered detrimental to water resources in Cebu. As was discussed at the conference,

Keidanren also provided effective support for NGO leaders in Japan as they fought for the passage of NPO legislation that would facilitate the incorporation process of nonprofit organizations, and was particularly helpful in lobbying influential conservative politicians.[6]

REQUIREMENTS FOR EFFECTIVE CORPORATE-NGO PARTNERSHIP

STATEMENT OF CORPORATE PHILOSOPHY FOR COMMUNITY INVOLVEMENT

One distinct commonality among most of the cases studied in this project is the clear statement of an organizational philosophy and values that emphasize the importance of corporate philanthropy in general and community involvement in particular.

Levi Strauss & Co. adopted a mission and aspiration statement to reinforce the company's commitment to the community. It asserts, "We will conduct our business ethically and demonstrate leadership in satisfying our responsibilities to our communities and the society." Eschewing the "compliance-based approach" of rules and regulations, Levi Strauss & Co. has instead opted for a "values-oriented approach" that emphasizes six ethical principles: honesty, promise keeping, fairness, respect for others, compassion, and integrity.

British Petroleum published a booklet in 1998, titled "What We Stand For . . .," which outlines a set of corporate values that should be manifested in corporate behavior. It spells out the corporation's business policies, emphasizing that "our policy commitments are the foundation on which we will build and conduct our business." In particular, it states that "those commitments are to be carried out by understanding the needs and aspirations of individuals, customers, contractors, suppliers, partners, governments, and nongovernmental organizations" and "by fulfilling obligations as a member of the societies in which BP operates."

Bankers Trust's guiding philosophy of "public responsibility and concern" recognizes a responsibility to the company's shareholders, customers, and employees and, at the same time, to the communities around the world in which it does business.

Keidanren announced its Global Environmental Charter in 1991, which

6. Details regarding this episode are provided in Tadashi Yamamoto, ed., *Deciding the Public Good: Governance and Civil Society in Japan* (Tokyo: Japan Center for International Exchange), 1999.

not only acknowledges that corporations are responsible for environmental degradation but also sets environmental standards for Japanese
corporate activities both in Japan and abroad.

Yasuda Kasai established a "Fundamental Policy on Environmental
Issues" in 1994, which was then adopted as the Yasuda Fire and Marine
Global Environment Charter in July 1998. This Charter not only commits
the company to supporting social contribution activities and environmental education but also calls upon employees to volunteer for environmental conservation and other efforts.

Toyota's Vision Theme for 2005, adopted in 1996 as a vision for the next
decade, focuses on "harmonious growth" and stresses harmony with
the global environment, with the global economy, with the company's
various stakeholders, and with the local communities in which the company operates.

COMMITMENT OF CORPORATE LEADERS

The above mission statements set forth by the corporations covered in
this case studies project might easily have remained nothing more than
noble goals or hollow rhetoric if it were not for the strong leadership
provided by senior executives of these organizations. The case study reports indicate that these statements are indeed buttressed by the personal commitments of senior corporate officers to achieving these stated
objectives.

One example of effective leadership is the case of Robert Haas, chief
exeutive officer of Levi Strauss & Co. Along with senior managers, he
joined employees in staffing booths and distributing literature on AIDS to
other employees at a time when little was known about the disease, and
when the stigma attached to it was still prevalent. Another example of
the impact of leadership was when Gaishi Hiraiwa, upon becoming the
chairman of Keidanren, introduced his philosophy of "*kyosei*," or "symbiosis," to the organization and its members, stressing the importance of
coexistence between corporations and the surrounding natural environment. Hiraiwa personally lobbied members for the adoption of an Environmental Charter, which was translated into action in 1992 when the
Keidanren Nature Conservation Fund was established to engage Keidanren member companies in nature conservation projects. At British Petroleum, leadership came not just from one individual but from 350 of the
company's top managers, who were involved in the drafting of the company's booklet, "What We Stand For. . . ."

Of course, while such individual leadership and involvement of up-per management is undoubtedly essential, the written statements of corporate philosophy and values are equally important to ensuring con-tinuity because, as an executive of Yasuda Kasai pointed out, "top man-agement is bound to change at some point in the future."

INVOLVING EMPLOYEES FOR CLOSE COOPERATION WITH COMMUNITIES

Several corporations in the case studies also emphasized the importance of disseminating or sharing such corporate philosophies with their em-ployees. British Petroleum's booklet on its corporate values was intended to reinforce the potential benefit of community relationships to its em-ployees, and a special effort was made to disseminate it to all of the com-pany's employees around the world. In addition, a video was prepared to accompany the booklet, and a small group of experts visited company of-fices to discuss the booklet with employees.

By ensuring that corporate philosophies and values are conveyed to all employees, companies are able to promote greater employee involvement in their community activities. This is a critical point since, as analyzed in this project, strong employee involvement appears to be a common fea-ture of successful community involvement activities by corporations. Participation by employees in such partnership activities enables corpo-rations to address the needs in their communities as they are perceived by people from the communities themselves, and reinforces the corpora-tions' commitment to community involvement. Employee participation also helps corporations project a community-friendly image. Moreover, employees gain a sense of pride, particularly if they are from the commu-nities where their corporations are promoting such activities.

Many of the companies studied here noted the educational benefits of employee involvement as well. Yasuda Kasai, for example, believes that encouraging employees to volunteer for environmental conservation ac-tivities not only is beneficial to the environment but also provides a learn-ing opportunity for employees. For its development project, Bankers Trust chose a neighborhood close to Metro Manila rather than a more remote rural location, with the specific goal of allowing its local employees—from clerical staff to the head of the country office—to go on site visits. Bankers Trust finds that such visits enable its staff to broaden their skills. Similarly, British Petroleum uses site visits as a part of its staff training strategy to teach employees about community development.

There seem to be diverse patterns of employee involvement in corporate community involvement activities. Bankers Trust's local staff helped villagers with business plans and provided technical assistance that allowed local residents to build new roads and other infrastructure on their own. Through the Glorious Cause efforts to alleviate poverty in China, employees of Chinese corporations often become involved as project coordinators and technical advisors for local partner organizations. Yasuda Kasai employees are involved in the planning and logistics of the environmental lecture series that the company conducts in partnership with an NGO. In addition, employees are encouraged to participate in local community events, and local branch managers are encouraged to become members of NGOs in their area.

ORGANIZATIONAL MECHANISMS
FOR EFFECTIVE COMMUNITY INVOLVEMENT

Some companies, such as Levi Strauss & Co., have elaborate organizational mechanisms to encourage employees to be active in their communities. Levi Strauss's Community Involvement Teams (CITs) organize workers throughout the company into groups of volunteers, offering them start-up money and matching the group's own fund-raising efforts. CITs are free to carry out their activities as they see fit within the broad guidelines set out by the corporation. Yasuda Kasai has established a "volunteer leave" system that allows workers to apply for up to three years of paid leave to work for nonprofit organizations. Yasuda Kasai is also an example of a company that has worked to systematically incorporate its philosophy of environmental protection into its daily corporate activities. It has established an ECO Committee within the corporation that seeks to promote energy conservation within the company, community involvement in environmental activities outside the company, and environment-related insurance goods and services as a part of the company's business operations.

EFFECTIVE COMMUNICATION BETWEEN CORPORATE
AND NGO PARTNERS

What was impressive about all the cases studied in this project was that there seem to have been concerted efforts on both sides of the partnership arrangements to communicate with each other in order to carry out joint tasks effectively. As mentioned above, the involvement of corporate staff at the ground level of operations obviously facilitates effective sharing of objectives and mutual understanding of the means to achieve them. As Barnett Baron pointed out in the concluding session of the Tokyo conference, it is critically important from the beginning of the partnership arrangement to focus on the desired outcomes, including which stakeholders and constituencies the partners are aiming to serve, and how to measure the outcome of such activity.

Several speakers at the conference pointed out that NGO leaders can sometimes be self-centered and self-righteous, assuming that they alone represent moral values and that corporations are not legitimate social actors. Clearly, it is essential for corporations and NGOs to develop mutual respect and confidence. As Rory Tolentino reminded the audience, corporate and NGO partners do not necessarily go into partnership with shared values. As was the case with the partnership between PT Aqua Golden Mississippi and the NGO Dana Mitra Lingkungan—which resulted from the NGO's criticism of the corporation for contributing to environmental pollution—some partnerships may actually find their point of departure in a clash of interests. Nevertheless, it is critical for both sides to establish an effective communications process through which they can develop a shared set of objectives and an understanding of the means to achieve them as they decide to forge a meaningful partnership. Such effective and continued communication between the partners also should make it possible for them to monitor and evaluate their joint work.

It should be pointed out, however, that as a result of the relative absence of professional expertise within NGOs in Asia, it is not always easy to develop effective communication in a short period of time. Intermediary organizations that have the confidence of both the corporate and NGO partners can play a critical role in developing such a communication process and, eventually, mutual trust.

EFFECTIVE USE OF INTERMEDIARIES

Several illustrations in the previous sections already point to the utility of NGOs as intermediaries in reaching out to a broader range of organizations and individuals in the communities, or as facilitators of community involvement activities. JCIE is one example of an NGO that plays this special role, often in close cooperation with its affiliate organization, the Asian Community Trust, and Philippine Business for Social Progress also has a specific mission as an intermediary. Many business associations also take on this intermediary role. The Keidanren Nature Conservation Fund serves as an intermediary organization between Japanese corporations interested in funding overseas environmental projects and environmental NGOs seeking corporate funding. The Federation of Korean Industries has started playing an active role in facilitating partnership with NGOs. The Glorious Cause in China has also played an intermediary role by helping more than 2,000 private entrepreneurs provide Rmb52 billion (US$6.24 billion at Rmb1 = US$0.12) in seed money and another Rmb400 million (US$48 million) in donations for 3,000 projects since its establishment in 1997.

Corporations seeking to start community involvement activities may be well served by such intermediaries that have professional expertise and special missions to play such a role. A leader of Keidanren's Committee on Corporate Philanthropy noted that one major reason for Japanese corporations' relative absence of community involvement activities in Asian countries is lack of knowledge of NGOs. The concept of using intermediaries is thus appealing to Keidanren members, although they feel a need to better understand the possibilities before pursuing such a path. For example, they would like to study the types of intermediaries that exist, the potential roles that they can play, the possible division of labor between corporations and intermediaries, and so on.

BUILDING PARTNERSHIP WITH THE PUBLIC SECTOR

One final and important prerequisite for effective corporate-NGO partnership at the community level is the development of a close working relationship with the local authorities. As corporations commit themselves to promoting the interests of communities, such relationships are both useful and natural. To have the support of the government, be it active or tacit, is important for effective corporate-NGO partnership, because governments have the ultimate capability to create an enabling environment for nonprofit organizations. Governments have the authority to determine the incorporation and registration processes, fiscal and tax treatment, and other factors that can serve as incentives or disincentives for partnerships.

In the case of British Petroleum, for example, one of the basic principles of the corporation's community affairs program is the establishment of partnerships with government authorities. This is particularly true of their activities in Vietnam, where it is necessary for foreign corporations and foreign NGOs to receive government approval for their operations and programs. In China, with the recent shift toward greater decentralization, the government has become increasingly aware of, and more receptive to, the creation of new relationships between the corporate sector, the nongovernmental sector, and local communities. It has encouraged and facilitated the work of corporations involved in community development as part of the All-China Federation of Industry and Commerce's initiative, the Glorious Cause. As noted above, in the case of the Cebu Hillyland Development Program, the mayor of Cebu City actually served as initiator and intermediary in the creation of the partnership.

It is evident from these cases that corporate-NGO partnerships are often actually developing in the broader context of multisectoral partnership, involving government authorities, media, community organizations, and people in the community. The involvement of a wider range of actors is an important and necessary trend that can make corporate-NGO partnerships even more productive. This, however, creates a more complex and challenging process for corporate and NGO leaders.

CONCLUSION

Given the limited sampling included in these case studies, it is difficult to form any definitive conclusions about the present scope and future prospects of corporate-NGO partnership in Asia Pacific. Nonetheless, some very general conclusions may be drawn from the studies and the Tokyo conference discussion, which may provide those interested in the subject with some new insights about the specific dynamics that present themselves in launching and implementing corporate-NGO partnerships.

One finding is that although the number of corporate-NGO partnerships may still be limited in Asia Pacific, there is a definite indication of their growing importance. The very productive interaction that took place at the Tokyo conference among business and NGO leaders is one clear sign of the increasing interest among corporations and NGOs in such arrangements. The changing context in the region favors further development of these partnerships. For one thing, there has been a dramatic emergence of civil society in Asian countries, and expectations for it to play an active role are rising in the wake of the financial crisis in the region. Corporations, on the other hand, are under pressure to contribute more positively to the overall interests of communities where they operate and also to improve corporate governance, the shortcomings of which have been regarded as one of the causes of the recent financial crisis.

Second, and related to the above point, the case studies indicate that the most significant aspect of these partnerships between corporations and NGOs is the synergy that is created as the partners bring their complementary talents and resources to the table. NGOs contribute to the partnerships a sense of values and an appreciation of the broader interests of the community (neither of which come easily to for-profit corporations), thus making corporations more conscious of the need to reorient themselves to meet the interests of their diverse stakeholders. Corporations bring not only financial resources and practical skills but also a sense of accountability and a focus on results, which are often lacking in their NGO counterparts.

A third general observation that can be made is that the changing dynamics surrounding corporations and NGOs reflect an environment in which much greater partnership among divergent sectors of society is needed to cope with fundamental shifts in society that have been brought about by the formidable forces of globalization. It can be said, on the basis of this case studies project, that corporate-NGO partnerships generally operate within broader multisectoral partnerships involving governments, intellectual and academic leaders, media, and members of the community. Although a great deal of attention has recently been paid to the role of intermediaries in partnership building, what is particularly striking is that, as partnerships evolve and incorporate actors from diverse sectors of society, all partners act in a sense as intermediaries, bringing their respective resources, experiences, and networks to the table as they work toward a common goal.

Fourth is that corporate-NGO partnerships take diverse patterns, and thus there is no simple model for success. Even the motivations of corporations for forming partnerships with NGOs, for example, seem to be quite divergent, as was manifest in the active debate on the subject at the Tokyo conference. Some corporations regard community involvement and partnership with NGOs as a part of their core business strategy, while others clearly prefer to promote it in the context of their pursuit of improved corporate governance and a new corporate identity. Nevertheless, certain criteria, as enumerated in the previous section, should be taken into account in bringing about effective partnerships.

A fifth general observation to be made is that, despite the positive prospects for corporate-NGO partnership in Asia Pacific as discussed earlier, such arrangements will face several major challenges in the coming years. One is the relatively weak institutional base of NGOs in Asia, caused by the limitations in financial and human resources. Another is the urgent need to enhance the enabling environment for NGOs by improving the legal, fiscal, and administrative contexts for their incorporation and activities, which are still constrained in most countries of East Asia. At this stage of civil society's development, corporate partnerships with NGOs necessarily have to address these problems of NGO infrastructure.

Sixth, perhaps the most critical requirement for bringing about a greater number of effective corporate-NGO partnerships in Asia Pacific is to do away with the traditional "us against them" attitude that remains between corporations and NGOs. Efforts are needed to further dismantle the lingering lack of trust between the two sectors, although there are encouraging signs on both sides that these exclusionary attitudes are beginning to break down. As evidenced by the Tokyo conference participants, a new breed of corporate manager is emerging who has had some experience working with NGOs as a student or corporate volunteer, and, conversely, an increasing number of NGO leaders have corporate backgrounds.

Seventh, as many participants in the Tokyo conference pointed out, there is growing recognition that regular forums and mechanisms are needed for continuing discussion between corporate and NGO leaders in order to promote greater mutual understanding and mutual trust between the two sectors. Corporations and NGOs naturally have different perspectives on diverse issues, and they speak "different languages." The Asia Pacific Philanthropy Consortium, the Council on Foundations of the United States, CIVICUS, Synergos, the Prince of Wales Business Forum, and JCIE have been holding a number of conferences that bring together corporate and NGO representatives. Industrial associations such as Keidanren and the Federation of Korean Industries have also started playing a role in facilitating dialogue between businesses and NGOs within their own countries, and with overseas counterparts. American Express has played a unique role in promoting such contact and dialogue between business corporations and NGOs by holding a series of meetings in Indochina. These meetings can also play a useful role in providing initial contact between potential partners, as exemplified in some of the cases studied in this project.

Finally, the case studies project and the Tokyo conference discussion reinforced a strong belief among the multinational researchers who worked together on the project that partnership of any kind depends in the final analysis on people who see the importance and joy of working together. The Tokyo conference offered an example of how corporate and NGO leaders throughout the region are increasingly coming together to explore ways of achieving partnership arrangements. Such joint efforts themselves will undoubtedly contribute to greater solidarity among people in different sectors who believe that civil society, working in concert with the corporate and public sectors, has an important role to play in dealing with the increasingly complex social issues within countries and the common issues facing the region and the world. It is the hope of those who have contributed to this project that its outcome will prove useful for organizations and individuals who are interested in forming future corporate-NGO partnerships.

2 Peduli Aqua–DML Program

Eka Budianta

IN 1993, a major Indonesian beverage company, PT Aqua Golden Mississippi (AGM), joined forces with Dana Mitra Lingkungan (DML, or Friends of the Environment), an environmental nongovernmental organization (NGO), to create a recycling program that would respond to the growing environmental hazard posed by discarded polyethelyne terephthalate (PET) bottles. That initiative, known as the Peduli Aqua–DML Program, ran for more than five years and involved local environmental NGOs and small entrepreneurs. While the program yielded mixed results, it was nonetheless a ground-breaking effort in Indonesia. It represented a substantial contribution by a domestic corporation to the field of environmental philanthropy, and was a model for partnerships between corporations and NGOs.

BACKGROUND

PT AQUA GOLDEN MISSISSIPPI

The moniker *Indonesia* is a word created by a British ethnologist to name the scattered islands between Asia and Australia. It was a translation of "*Tanahair*," a local idiom used to signify homeland. "*Tanah*" was translated into Latin as "*nesos*," or land; "*air*" was translated as "*indos*," meaning water. In other words, "Indos-nesos," or Indonesia, means "The Land of Water." It is ironic that a bottled water company should find success in Indonesia, where water seems to be so plentiful. Nonetheless, drinking water has always been, and may always be, a problem for most places in the archipelago.

The Indonesian drinking water industry began in 1973, after the foreign guest of a corporate lawyer became ill as a result of drinking unhealthy tap water at the five-star hotel where she was staying. This incident inspired that lawyer, Tirto Utomo, to find a way to provide healthy drinking water for the luxury hotels in Jakarta. He founded a new company, PT Aqua Golden Mississippi, named after North America's longest river. According to Utomo's successor, Willy Sidharta, the name was chosen because Mississippi means the "father of water." Within a year, the company had introduced drinking water packaged in glass bottles and marketed under the name "Aqua." The water was sold not only to luxury hotels but to the general public as well.

AGM's success opened the door for competitors, too, and in less than two decades more than 50 different brands of bottled drinking water had sprung up across Indonesia. Nonetheless, AGM continued to lead the market with more than one billion liters of drinking water produced each year. AGM's Aqua was sold within Indonesia and throughout the Asia Pacific region, and Aqua managed to become the "official drink" of national and international events in Southeast Asia.

THE PROBLEM OF SOLID WASTE

As sales grew, however, so too did the problem of waste. Bottles were scattered everywhere, littering the streets of Jakarta and mountains and beaches as well.

In 1981, the polyvinyl chloride plastic bottle was introduced. The advantage of this bottle was that it could easily be recycled and turned into such products as plastic pipes, ropes, jars, garbage pails, and clothes hangers. Unfortunately, it also had a number of drawbacks: It was relatively heavy; the smell of the plastic tainted the drinking water; and the production and recycling of polyvinyl chloride produced a toxic smoke.

For these reasons the new plastic PET was introduced in 1987. PET is clean, clear, lightweight, safe, and odorless. It was therefore an excellent container for drinking water, and its use provided a significant boost to the bottled drinking water market. The drawbacks are that the PET plastic waste makes soil less fertile and is estimated to take more than a century to decompose. PET plastic waste is not reusable and cannot be made into new bottles. It can, however, be crushed and made into flakes or plastic fiber, which can then be sold for use in carpets, curtains, polyester fabrics, and toys. Unfortunately, at that time these potential uses were not well understood in Indonesia, and PET bottles were not being recycled.

Environmentalist and consumer rights activist Erna Witoelar was quick to bring this issue to the attention of Utomo, whom she knew through their participation in the nonprofit organization DML. As early as 1988, she began to criticize Aqua for the amount of waste that it was producing. Utomo took this criticism by Witoelar and other environmentalists seriously and began to look into the issue.

Utomo was considered to be environmentally conscious in running his business operations. In the late 1980s, for example, he became aware that the use of deep wells for obtaining water was not environmentally sustainable. As a result, he quickly shifted the company to spring water, purchasing not only the springs but also the land surrounding the springs to protect parts of the water catchment area. This became an asset for marketing as well, since Aqua was able to boast in its advertising campaigns of "the taste of fresh, natural mountain spring water from well-protected sources located in the beautiful mountains throughout Indonesia." In recognition of his efforts, a local NGO awarded Utomo the Sahwali Award in 1991.

In 1992, during a debate at a public seminar on the environment held to address the issue of urban solid waste, Utomo promised Witoelar and others in attendance that he would find a solution to the PET bottle problem within a year. True to his word, on February 1, 1993, Utomo invited Witoelar and the state minister of the environment, Emil Salim, to AGM's Ciracas factory on the southern outskirts of Jakarta to witness the launching of the Peduli Aqua–DML recycling program.

THE PEDULI AQUA–DML PROGRAM

Utomo had responded quickly to the criticism lodged against his company, and had actively sought methods of educating the public and promoting the recycling of PET bottles. He traveled abroad to view PET recycling efforts in other countries, studying such examples as Germany, Taiwan, Japan, and the United States before devising his strategy. The program that he eventually developed consisted of two primary components: a "buy-back" plan to encourage consumers to return used bottles, and the distribution of crusher machines to turn the plastic into a usable form for recycling.

To put the plan into effect, AGM turned to DML, a nonprofit organization with an extensive network of environmental NGOs and environmentally concerned businesses. Utomo chose to work with DML in this venture because he trusted the people involved and had good business relations with a number of DML's founders. Together, the two organizations created the Peduli Aqua–DML Program, which ran from 1993 to 1998. Sadly, Utomo did not live to see the fruits of his efforts. He suffered a heart attack in 1994 and passed away at the age of 64. Nonetheless, the company continued its commitment to the Peduli program for several more years.

THE BUY-BACK PROGRAM

The Indonesian word "*peduli*" literally means "concern," but it was also used as an abbreviation of "Program Daur Ulang Limbah," or "waste recycling program." The Peduli Aqua–DML logo was printed on all 600-milliliter and 1,500-milliliter bottles of Aqua water. Consumers paid a Rp10 (Rp4,375 = US$1 as of December 1997) deposit for the large bottle, and a Rp5 deposit on the smaller size. When they returned the bottles, they would be reimbursed twice the cost of the deposit. Unfortunately, that amount was not significant enough to represent a real incentive for most consumers. Drinking water in major Indonesian cities is more expensive than gasoline. In 1997, for example, a liter of bottled water was selling for Rp1,200 (US$0.26) as compared to Rp700 (US$0.15) for a liter of gasoline. For those who could afford the water, the promise of Rp10 or Rp20 in return for the bottles was not compelling. As a result, few bottles were returned and the waste problem continued to worsen. In 1995, for example, a report from researchers working in Jakarta Bay noted that a large number of empty Aqua bottles were scattered in the sea and were threatening the mangrove plants along the shore.

It quickly became clear that the program would not be successful without the help of scavengers or garbage pickers, locally known as *pemulung*. For these people, the Rp10–20 represented a more significant amount. The scavengers were led by coordinators known as *pelapak*, and they gathered not just plastic bottles but any kind of garbage that might have economic value. Lisa Utomo, Tirto's wife, accompanied the AGM and DML program staff on visits to several islands to help recruit *pemulung* to participate in the program. H. Hartono, an energetic AGM manager who was assigned to coordinate the Peduli Aqua program, conducted several training workshops to teach the *pemulung* how to choose, clean, and sell the PET bottles to a *pelapak*. A number of *pelapak* established a close relationship with AGM, which in turn gave them trucks to pick up the collected bottles. In 1993 alone, AGM management claimed that almost 30 percent of the bottles sold were returned and recycled. (The number of bottles returned to retailers decreased in subsequent years as a result of increased access to crushing facilities run by the Peduli program and others.)

THE CRUSHER DISTRIBUTION PROGRAM

Once the bottles were collected, the next step was to turn them into a recyclable form. The main challenge for the Peduli program was how to distribute crushing machines to interested parties as a way of involving the communities in the process and promoting small-scale enterprises. More than 20 machines were distributed around the country as grants over the first three years of the program, and an additional six machines were distributed in the final two years, even though the price had nearly tripled after 1997 as a result of the devalued currency. The machines consist of an engine, a washer to clean the bottles, and a container with steel blades to crush the plastic into flakes. The machine creates a thundering noise, which means that the ideal locale is far away from housing and close enough to a river for a water supply. To run the machine requires two operators and a supply of plastic bottles to crush. Anyone who could provide adequate space and manpower was able to request a crusher.

A small machine is capable of crushing 200 kilograms of plastic a day, while a large machine can turn 500 kilograms of clean bottles into flakes. The flakes were sold primarily to textile factories. The program assisted in the marketing of the flakes, although those with the crushers were free to sell their flakes to anyone they chose. The price of the crushed bottles was between Rp300 (US$0.06) and Rp500 (US$0.11) per kilogram, while the price of flakes ranged from Rp600 (US$0.13) to Rp1,500 (US$0.33). The actual earnings depended on the cleanliness of the bottles and the price fluctuations for the reground flakes, but most of the ventures succeeded in making a profit.

The program director from AGM and the executive director of DML were responsible for selecting the recipients of the crushers. They traveled to various cities to explain the program to the public, monitor the program, and participate in various events concerning waste recycling and water conservation. Drawing on the support of its network of environmentalists, DML often requested the collaboration of local NGOs to assist in overseeing the program. To select a nongovernmental organization, DML would usually ask for a recommendation from the Wahana Lingkungan Hidup Indonesia, the largest forum of Indonesian environmentalists, supported by more than 350 NGOs. The NGOs generally served as a mediator between the crusher owner and the funder (DML), as well as between the crusher owner and the flake buyer. The NGOs also assisted the crusher owners in maintaining and operating the machines.

The money earned from the deposits and the profits from selling the crushed PET plastic was channeled into the Peduli Aqua–DML Program. A total of Rp3.55 billion (US$811,429) was donated by AGM over the five-year program to the fund administered by DML. That included Rp2 billion (US$248,447 at Rp8,050 = US$1 as of December 1998) given to DML in December 1998, after the Peduli recycling program had officially ended. It should be noted that interest rates were very high in Indonesia, and thus the endowment earned anywhere from 20 percent annually under normal conditions to up to 60 percent per year during the financial crisis that began in the country in 1998. Thus DML was earning at least Rp700 million (US$160,000) per year on its endowment.

In addition to covering the buy-back and recycling programs, the Peduli Aqua–DML Program supported a variety of environmental efforts through grants to NGOs, student organizations, and local governments. From 1994 to 1998, a total of Rp200 million (US$45,714) was distributed to more than 60 grantees for public awareness outreach, exhibitions, seminars, and environmental campaigns. Some funds were used to support activities conducted by DML.

DANA MITRA LINGKUNGAN

DML was established in 1983 to increase environmental awareness among leaders of industry and to promote corporate philanthropy by encouraging donations for nature conservation and environmental education. Most members of DML are businesspeople from the banking, public relations, and manufacturing sectors. Other members include professors, government ministers, retired generals, and NGO activists. PT Aqua Golden Mississippi was one of the early supporters of the organization, although it was not a founding member. In return for their participation in DML, member businesses gain the reputation of being environmentally conscious companies, or "friends of the environment."

This title does not come easily, and DML has been known to have turned down offers of donations from companies with bad environmental track records.

DML's activities incorporate two primary functions. First, DML serves as a grant-making organization. From its founding in 1983 until the establishment in 1994 of a new institution called the Biodiversity Foundation, DML was in fact the only environmental funding agency in Indonesia. Acting as an intermediary, DML mobilizes funds from business and industry to help NGOs in the field. In its first 15 years, DML channeled more than Rp1.5 billion (US$342,857) in funds to more than 100 projects in 23 of the 27 provinces in the Republic of Indonesia. The projects ranged from medicinal plant conservation to the founding of a survival school in the jungle. A significant portion of the funds was spent on the promotion of sanitation through the building of 34 public toilets along rivers throughout the country's capital city, Jakarta. DML also maintained partnerships with the United Nations Development Program in channeling US$600,000 of Global Environmental Facilities small grants to NGOs during a pilot phase between 1994 and 1997.

As part of the Peduli Aqua–DML Program, as noted above, DML used a portion of the funds raised to make grants to NGOs and for student activities. Among the largest grants made with the Peduli funds was a 1997 gift of Rp20 million (US$4,571) to the Garuda Nusantara Foundation, led by Ully Sigar Rusady, a well-known singer and a United Nations Environmental Program Global 500 Awardee. Rusady was known to AGM because Utomo had once requested that she compose a jingle for an Aqua advertisement. The project funded was to provide radio transmitters and receivers to local governments and individuals living on the remote islands in the southeast Sulawesi waters.

The second function of DML is to conduct its own activities, such as regular breakfast and luncheon meetings to disseminate information to the business community on cleaner production, energy conservation, and pollution control. DML is also involved in the publication of posters, cards, brochures, bulletins, and newsletters.

Another set of activities that DML funds and oversees is aimed at promoting nature conservation. For example, Peduli funds helped finance a Javan tiger expedition conducted in 1996–1997 in the Meru Betiri jungle of East Java. The goal was to confirm whether Javan tigers still existed or were truly extinct and, if they did exist, to promote the preservation of the area as a natural heritage site. The expedition did find credible proof that the tigers still exist, and was thus able to help in the fight against the penetration of agro-industries into the area.

Yet another regular program of DML is environmental networking. There are several forums and networks supported by DML, including the Clean Ciliwung Movement to clean up 13 rivers within the special district of Jakarta, the Cleaner Production Roundtable, the Business Council for Sustainable Development, and the Indonesian Environmental Education Network. The latter, a forum of more than 40 NGOs, received Peduli support for its first directory on environmental education and business centers in 1998, while the Clean Ciliwung Movement received a boat for patrolling the river from the Peduli Aqua–DML Program. In addition to overseeing DML's grants, dues, and manpower, the organization's executive director is actively involved in a number of these efforts, being a founding member of the Clean Ciliwung Movement, editor-in-chief of the Ciliwung magazine, and a Steering Committee member of the Indonesian Environmental Education Network.

From 1998, DML also began working with the United States Asia Environmental Partnership to promote a campaign for cleaner production in business and industry. This program focuses on small-scale businesses, providing training and technical assistance on a consulting basis to help these companies lessen the environmental impact of their manufacturing and other activities.

IMPACT OF THE PEDULI PROGRAM ON DML

The effect of the Peduli program on DML was substantial, particularly given the scale and timing. The early to mid-1990s was understandably a difficult period for environmental funding in Indonesia, given the state of the economy at the time. AGM was the only major donor to DML for about five years. Companies that had previously given generously to DML, such as Bank Central Asia, Astra, Lippo, Bank Niaga, Unilever, and Indomobil, either went bankrupt or chose to suspend their support. DML narrowly averted losing substantial portions of its funds when two of the banks holding DML funds went bankrupt. In one case, a founder of DML, William Soeryadjaya, happened to be a co-owner of the liquidated bank, so the fund was saved just a few hours before all assets of the bank were frozen. In this context, AGM's support was even more remarkable.

When Utomo made his promise to clean up his company's waste and donate the resulting funds to help environmental activities all across the country, there was nothing in writing that would obligate him to keep his word. The only written proof was a report of the 1992 seminar at which the promise was made. It is understandable, then, that the Board of Directors of DML was pleasantly surprised when AGM began its donations. The amount received in the first phase of the program was Rp200 million (US$45,714), roughly the same amount as the organization's annual budget at that time. Between 1994 and 1997, AGM presented DML with three payments amounting to more than Rp1.5 billion (US$342,857); a final, unexpected payment of Rp2 billion (US$248,447 at Rp8,050 = US$1 as of December 1998) was made in December 1998.

The expansion of DML's programs also led to a change in the structure of the organization. For more than ten years, it had relied on individual commitment, voluntary contributions, and the passion and ideas of the Board of Directors. The Board's 12 members contributed suggestions about how to finance projects, mobilize funds, and hold events. But in July 1994, the Board decided to hire a professional executive director to head the organization's activities. The executive director and his three staff worked closely with the AGM staff in running the Peduli program, making it a true partnership.

RATIONALE FOR THE PARTNERSHIP

The partnership with AGM clearly benefited DML. The NGO was able to get funds for its own operations at a time when funds for the environment were hard to come by, and it mobilized additional Peduli funds for distribution to environmental NGOs throughout Indonesia. In addition, it was able to influence AGM to become a more environmentally concerned company.

AGM, for its part, was able to address the serious environmental issue posed by its products and to improve its reputation as a "Friend of the Environment"; this status was publicized by the Peduli Aqua–DML labels attached to AGM's products. The grants to the NGOs highlighted AGM's efforts as well, and DML publications were able to portray AGM's work both in the Peduli program and in its other activities, such as a reforestation project it undertook in the areas near its fresh springs. It should be noted that there was no financial gain for AGM in terms of a tax deduction, since Indonesia does not have a system of tax exemption for donations to NGOs. The work of AGM for the environment should therefore be regarded as motivated by sincere concern and goodwill. Lisa Utomo believed that environmental philanthropy is an expression of gratitude to nature, and she encouraged DML to enhance its campaign to promote environmental awareness throughout Indonesian society.

THE END OF THE PROGRAM

AGM terminated the Peduli program as of July 1998. The people and organizations that had crushers continue their work as a regular business, and the PET bottles have become a kind of commodity, treated as the raw material for flake producers. Although the refund is no longer offered by AGM, the scavengers continue to collect the bottles and sell them to those businesses for Rp300–500 (US$0.04–0.06) per kilogram, depending on the cleanliness of the bottles.

While the reasons for terminating the program are not clear, there seem to have been a number of factors that might have contributed to this decision. Although AGM was the largest producer of water in Indonesia, and perhaps in the entire Asia Pacific region, the economic crisis of 1998 hit the company hard. It was forced to sell 40 percent of its shares to Danone, a major France-based food corporation, to help pay off its foreign debt. It is not certain whether these financial difficulties and the resultant merger factored into the decision to stop the program. Other explanations include the fact that PET recycling had become a regular business among plastic manufacturers, and in fact had become a competitive industry. As demand grew, the price paid for bottles rose, and the collection of PET bottles increased. These circumstances made the refund system unnecessary, since there was already a market for the empty bottles. In addition, the economic slowdown in Asia made the refund system difficult to sustain, since the basic price of the water was already considered to be extremely high for most consumers.

Later in 1998, AGM opened a new recycling plant. Although the Peduli program no longer existed, the crushing of tons of PET bottles continued. Two giant crushers, accompanied by two huge washing machines, were installed in a large compound in the Gunung Putri area, a few kilometers away from the old Aqua plant in Ciracas, where the Peduli program was inaugurated in 1993. As a symbol that the partnership between DML and AGM would continue, Lisa Utomo, now the owner of AGM and a Board member of DML, attended the plant's opening, handing the tip of a traditional mountain-shaped pile of rice to the executive director of DML just before the crushers began their loud roar. Unfortunately, by early 1999, that recycling plant had ceased operating as a result of a manpower crisis.

At least 100 out of AGM's roughly 7,000 employees were facing early retirement as part of a streamlining strategy.

There are signs, however, that the Peduli program succeeded in inspiring other initiatives. In October 1998, Coca-Cola began a similar program for recycling PET bottles, although instead of providing the crushers as grants, Coca-Cola provided them as a no-interest loan. Within AGM as well, there was an indication that the company was taking the issue of corporate philanthropy more seriously. In March 1999, PT Tirta Investama, the parent company of the Aqua Group, established its own foundation, and the staff of the Peduli Aqua program were reassigned to it. The main objective of the new foundation, the Friends of Aqua Foundation, is to promote the development of a healthy society and sustainable water resources.

CONCLUSION

EVALUATING THE PEDULI AQUA–DML PROGRAM

The environmental degradation in Indonesia is testament to the failure of numerous environmental campaigns launched by the government, NGOs, and the business sector over the years. It was clear that no one sector could achieve its goals alone; partnerships were needed to battle pollution. The PET recycling campaign, utilizing a corporate-NGO partnership, was successful not only in contributing to the protection of the soil from plastic waste but also in creating business ventures and generating income for thousands of scavengers and recyclers.

But the problem of PET pollution is beyond the capacity of this single program to fully address, and there are still large areas in Indonesia that are not covered by recycling programs. To make matters worse, the consumption of PET plastic has increased dramatically as its use in beverage and cooking oil containers has grown. It is now estimated that up to 30 million tons a year are being consumed in Indonesia.

While it is unreasonable to expect that this program alone could solve the PET plastic problem, a number of legitimate criticisms of the Peduli Aqua–DML Program can be raised. First, there is some question as to whether all of the funds generated by the buy-back and recycling initiatives were actually handed over from AGM to DML. The accounting was complicated by the extreme shifts in exchange rates during the period the program operated, and a full financial report on the program was delayed by the deaths of the program's treasurer and his assistant in short succession. One source asserted that the lack of sizable environmental protection programs conducted by DML had given AGM management an excuse for not presenting the entire fund to the designated NGO. It appears that almost the entire Rp3.55 billion (US$440,994) donation is still maintained as DML's endowment, except for a Rp100 million (US$12,442) donation that was made to the Wallacea Foundation for a marine research project. (After the financial crisis, the monthly interest earned on the endowment is well over Rp100 million, or US$12,442.) Whatever the facts, there was clearly a lack of transparency, an absence of public control, and inadequate information on the collected fund and its usage, both on the part of AGM and DML.

A second important issue was that AGM and DML failed to educate the general public adequately about the bottle refund system. According to the Indonesian Consumers Institute, the corporation and the NGO did not provide enough easily accessible locations where consumers could return their bottles. AGM responded to this complaint by distributing bottle bags and stands to its dealers, but not many had been used by the end of the program. As mentioned previously, the low refund amount was another factor that discouraged consumers from bringing the bottles back. A similar refund system in Germany, for example, used a deposit amount 20 times greater than the Rp5–10 deposit for the Aqua bottles. AGM did not feel that it could ask for any larger deposit, because Aqua was already the most expensive bottled water in the country.

A third problem, which was not disclosed until after the partnership ended, was DML's insufficient role in promoting the program. It was peculiar that although many of DML's supporters were public relations and advertising practitioners, none of them lent their expertise to promote public awareness of the PET recycling program. The only real publicity came at the beginning of the program, when AGM produced and televised a 60-second video clip introducing the refund program.

In short, while the partnership between AGM and DML was successful in many respects, it is clear that there was room for improvement.

THE FUTURE OF CORPORATE-NGO PARTNERSHIPS
IN INDONESIA

In the past, the absence of incentives and rules has been a stumbling block for corporate philanthropy in Indonesia, and the financial crisis compounded this problem. On the other hand, those corporations that survived have been overwhelmed by requests for donations to assist the poor. Social and economic recovery programs became everybody's concern during this period.

In the meantime, Indonesian NGOs entered a new phase of their history in 1998, with the ouster of General Suharto and the collapse of his New Order regime. Hundreds of new environmental and social organizations, political parties, and media organizations flowered in a way that was unthinkable prior to May 1998.

DML and other environmental NGOs benefited from an influx of international funding starting from the mid-1990s. In 1994, the Japanese and American governments established the Biodiversity Foundation with an initial endowment of US$20 million, which was more than 20 times larger than DML. Over 30 foreign environmental funding agencies, such as the Australian Agency for International Development (AusAid), Swiss Contact, Keidanren (Japan Federation of Economic Organizations), and the U.S. Agency for International Development (USAID), began to pour funds into Indonesia, and international environmental NGOs such as the World Wildlife Federation, Wetlands International, and The Nature Conservancy opened offices or programs in Indonesia as well.

Despite facing crises on various fronts, local and international nongovernmental organizations operating in Indonesia were in many ways enjoying greater freedom and financial support than ever before. The formerly closed society that had been so heavily controlled by the militaristic Suharto government was now open, and citizens moved quickly to promote a free market and a sustainable civil society. Given this context, corporations have been forced to abandon their "Santa Claus charity" attitude and adopt a more responsible approach to the country's social and economic recovery. Undoubtedly, this new environment will create greater opportunities for partnerships between corporations and NGOs. What type of partnership should be built and how such partnerships can be most effective are questions that remain to be answered.

3 Panmai Group Partnership

Paiboon Wattanasiritham
and
Anuchat Poungsomlee

I N the small, rural town of Baan Song Hong in Roi Et Province in north-east Thailand, a group of women created a community business organization known as the Panmai Group. Working together with a non-governmental organization (NGO) called the Appropriate Technology Association (ATA), the women began a cooperative focused on the weaving of traditional materials. The cooperative gradually evolved into a broad network for the production and retailing of clothing, as well as the operation of gasoline stands. Through these activities, the Panmai Group was able to contribute to the well-being of its members, the development of the community, and the empowerment of women as community leaders.

As the Panmai Group expanded, it increasingly worked in cooperation with other sectors of society, including both the government and business sectors. This type of multiparty partnership for community development, and particularly the involvement of the corporate sector, is a new phenomenon in Thailand. Accordingly, the experiences of the Panmai Group offer important lessons for future cooperative efforts in social and economic development.[1]

The authors gratefully acknowledge the assistance of Arphorn Chansomwong and Pam Tansagnuanwong.

1. The philanthropic environment described in this chapter was typical before the Asian financial and economic crisis started in 1997. At that time, the business sector had the capacity to be involved in and to contribute to social development projects with other sectors. The crisis, however, forced many companies to shut down operations and many

PHILANTHROPIC ACTIVITIES
OF THAILAND'S BUSINESS SECTOR

EVOLUTION OF THE BUSINESS SECTOR'S ROLE
IN SOCIETY

The philanthropic activities of Thailand's business sector started more than 20 years ago, and in the ensuing decades such activities have played a growing role in social and economic development. The initial philanthropic organization was an association of ethnic Chinese businesspeople that provided social welfare programs for its members. This association subsequently evolved into trade associations that played an important role in the development of the Thai economic sector.

Over the next decade, companies and business groups provided social services to their members, employees, and the community, but only in a limited capacity. Efforts to increase the role of corporations in society first appeared during the administration of General Prem Tinnasulanondha, when the government appointed a Joint Public and Private Sectors Committee in 1981 to promote collaboration between the public and private sectors for the purpose of national development. Similar committees were also created at the provincial level. The real turning point, however, was the "Rural Development Plan" of the Fifth National Economic and Social Development Plan (1982–1986). Under this plan, the government mobilized various resources to help develop communities at the district and village levels, and initiated diverse forms of development activities that involved civic leaders, private organizations, and community organizations. This period also saw a marked increase in the awareness of development issues among the educated middle class, which led to the formation of volunteer groups and NGOs that began taking an active part in rural development. These groups and organizations formed the basis for today's community organizations working in rural development.

During the late 1980s, which coincided with the Sixth National Economic and Social Development Plan (1987–1991), the government revised the country's economic policy to focus on industrial development, with the goal of Thailand attaining the status of a newly industrialized country. Unfortunately, the economic success of this period brought with

others to tighten their budgets and cut their support for social causes. Some socially minded businesses and individual businesspeople have continued their support for social development projects in a nonfinancial manner, providing their expertise and time.

it a number of negative impacts as well. People in rural communities and in the general public began to see the linkage between business investment and a deterioration in natural resources and the environment; this insight led to a backlash against industry. In response, many corporations began to recognize the need to make greater efforts to give back to society.

The economic and social changes during this period resulted in the creation of a number of movements led by the private sector, local organizations, and NGOs and which focused on rural development and environmental protection. These movements can be considered as the beginning of the private sector's involvement in the process of national development at the policy level. One of the changes that the movement accomplished, for example, was the initiation of public hearings on the implementation of development projects. This was the result of efforts by middle-class individuals involved in NGO development work and by private companies involved in financing various NGO development projects.

During this period, business-NGO collaboration in development projects was still in its nascent phase. Most NGO activities were conducted directly with local communities, while the business sector was more involved with development at the policy level, and thus had a limited role in rural and social development.

In the 1990s, the imbalance in economic development between rural and urban areas in Thailand, and between developed and developing countries in Asia, deepened the already existing social problems in Thailand and exacerbated ties with neighboring countries. The challenges facing the country include AIDS, trafficking in women and children, drugs, poverty, and the environment.

Awareness of environmental and development issues in Thai society seems to have been defined as a middle-class phenomenon, in which the business sector has played an important role. The emergence of business organizations and businesspeople that were willing to take a public stand on the environment and sustainable development was clearly a new social phenomenon in recent years. These organizations and individuals sought to demonstrate that business practice and production methods that promote environmental protection and sustainable development were indeed possible. The Regent Hotel, for example, worked with Mahidol University and the Local Development Institute (an NGO) to organize a pilot project in environmental development for the Regent

Hotel's Cha-Am Resort. And a group of finance companies formed a partnership with NGOs and community organizations to conduct a "community development reforestation" project in Nan Province. These projects not only represented a heightened consciousness among corporations but also demonstrated the potential for cooperation between the corporate sector and other sectors of society.

At present, a number of business groups are involved in social development or other philanthropic activities. In general, the companies or business organizations involved in these activities tend to be large organizations that have established some form of social assistance policy. Most of the activities either correspond to the underlying operational policies of those businesses or are carried out in the communities or target groups in which the business operates. The activities may take various forms, such as the allocation of budget to NGOs or the establishment of an independent foundation for social development. The prevalent format of businesses' social development activities, however, is still donations, and participation in development-oriented activities with communities remains a relatively rare phenomenon.

THE EVOLUTION TOWARD MULTIPARTY PARTICIPATION

As noted, the increasing socioeconomic problems of the 1990s have placed severe strains on Thai society as a whole, posing a serious challenge to sustainable development. It has become clear that traditional attitudes and approaches will not suffice to solve the various problems facing the country. Participation from all sectors in a collaborative effort to address these problems will be essential. This theme is echoed in the Eighth National Economic and Social Development Plan (1997–2001), which emphasizes "people" as the center of development and promotes a concept of multiparty participation that includes the public sector, the private business sector, NGOs, the mass media, academic institutions, and private citizens.

In the past, a number of projects have been initiated to mobilize the participation of the private business sector in partnership with the public sector and appropriate NGOs. These partnerships were focused mainly on activities concerning environmental protection or arts and culture, such as the renovation of the Klong Lod canal in Bangkok, the Pesticide-Free Agricultural Villages Project in Chachoengsao and Prachin Buri provinces, or the Green Label Project. However, as the government broadened the emphasis of its policies in response to shifting public opinion over the past five to six years, the private sector has been prodded to support a wider range of social development activities.

One reflection of this shift is the more widespread use of such terms as "corporate citizenship," "corporate social responsibility," and "corporate community involvement." These terms indicate the heightened participation of the private sector in the creation of a strong civil society. Within the competitive economic environment in Thailand, many corporate executives viewed community development as a competitive strategy, allowing them to foster the economic and social potential of the communities in which that business is operating as a way of contributing to their company's long-term success. This type of social support is thus considered to be a returning of profits to society and, at the same time, a long-term investment that reflects the objectives of the corporation.

As the corporate sector's attention shifted to greater community involvement, a second trend was under way that also bodes well for corporate-NGO, or multisectoral, partnerships. The nonprofit sector was growing, both in the scale and scope of its activities. Economic growth had made capital more available for NGOs, and—equally important— prosperity had spurred the expansion of the Thai middle class, along with its expectations and concerns regarding social inequality, the environment, and health and quality of life.

In response to these trends, several major organizations were established to encourage corporate partnerships with the nonprofit and other sectors. The Thailand Business Council for Sustainable Development, formed in 1993 by former Prime Minister Anand Panyarachun and leading Thai businesspeople, is aimed at supporting the private sector's leadership role in the prevention and solving of national environmental problems. The Thai Business Initiatives for Rural Development project, created within the Population and Community Development Association in 1986, mobilized capital and human resources from the private business sector to help the poor through various development projects that promote self-reliance. The latest movement illustrating the awareness of the private business sector in social development is the establishment of the Business Group for Thai Society (BGTS), which conducts seminars, study visits, and other activities. The group was formed at the initiative of Paiboon Wattanasiritham, the director of the Government Saving Bank, who began discussions with representatives from various industries. Coordination and academic support for the BGTS are provided by the Center for Phianthropy and Civil Society in the National Institute of Development Administration.

THE BUSINESS SECTOR'S ROLE IN THE DEVELOPMENT OF COMMUNITY BUSINESS

Another important element of the Thai development strategy was the concept of "community business," which became widely accepted and implemented during the period of the Eighth National Economic and Social Development Plan as a means of creating self-reliant communities. The goal of establishing these community businesses was to enable families and communities to participate in their own economic development. Attainment of that goal necessitated a joining of forces from every sector of society. The role of the business sector gradually evolved, and that sector is increasingly participating as a partner in development, applying its resources of capital, management, and marketing to support the development of community organizations and businesses.

Presently, many community organizations are conducting business-oriented activities in agriculture, handicrafts, and industry. These businesses are owned and operated by the community, usually in the form of cooperatives, and are supported by the public sector, the private business sector, and NGOs. The role of the private business sector in such activities is often that of providing purchase orders and assisting with marketing. The NGOs assume the role of advisor and coordinator between the community organizations and the private business sector.

Some examples of such cooperative arrangements include the Bata Shoe Factory project of the Nang Rong community in Bureerum Province, which was coordinated and supervised by the Population and Community Development Association; and the support by Bangchak Petroleum Public Co., Ltd., of the operations of the Lemon Green convenience stores and gas stations, run by more than 500 community organizations.

While these partnerships are promising, they are still in the early stages. Community businesses face many challenges, such as a lack of funding sources, a lack of management capabilities, and insufficient knowledge of marketing and business law. Moreover, the government has numerous regulations that inhibit the growth of private businesses. At present, however, the most pressing needs are for the creation of social capital to strengthen civil society and the promotion of cooperation between various groups to create a participatory process of social development. These will be the keys to achieving sound social and economic development that can lead to a good economy, good morals, and good politics.

The Panmai Group case presented here is an example of a civil society organization that formed to find a solution to the community's problems through the operation of a community business. The Panmai Group has successfully drawn on the strength of the nonprofit, business, and government sectors to help promote its community business.

THE PANMAI GROUP AND THE DEVELOPMENT OF A COMMUNITY BUSINESS

EVOLUTION OF THE PANMAI GROUP

In 1985, a group of women concerned with the problems facing their village, and with the role of women in particular, formed a community organization and approached a nongovernmental organization, ATA, for assistance. In the initial planning phase of the project, ATA and the women organized a series of discussions, study visits, and training. Consultations were held with the various stakeholders, including the women's husbands, in order to analyze the problems of the community and their causes.

It was perceived that the establishment of an alternative occupation to supplement the rural women's income would lead to an improvement in the quality of life both for the women and their families. In addition, if such an occupation could be pursued without the women leaving the village, it would alleviate the problem of migrant labor from the rural areas to the cities. A feasibility study indicated that the weaving of traditional materials, an activity in which the women of the northeastern provinces were already involved, was a potential activity around which the women could organize themselves. As a result, a project for the development of the weaving of traditional cotton and silk materials using natural dyes was initiated in Baan Song Hong, Kasetvisai District, Roi Et Province.

Initially, the project emphasized the production aspects of the weaving business, including research and development of techniques concerning color, patterns, and dyeing methods, so that the materials produced would be of improved quality. At the same time, there was an emphasis on community development, focusing on group organization, leadership development, and training in such areas as accounting and marketing. The main objective throughout the process was to instill the concept of self-reliance in the community. Members were involved in all levels of activity and decision making, from setting prices to determining invest-ments. A committee handled the management, and leadership was ro-tated to spread the responsibilities and create opportunities for leadership training.

The project expanded rapidly, resulting in the formation of a network known as the Panmai Group. Panmai is a multicolored plant, symbolic of the natural materials and dyes that the women were using in their tex-tiles. The main activity of the Group was the purchase and sale of ma-terials woven by the members. The goods that were produced had to meet standards and prices established jointly by the Group's members. In 1991, income generated per member averaged out to 4,410 baht (US$120 at US$1 = 36.65 baht), which increased to 9,996 baht (US$272.74) in 1997. From 1991, the Group expanded its activities from weaving to the production of clothing, and over time the Group developed a clear mar-keting system that included wholesale, consignment, and retail sales with domestic and foreign customers. In addition, the Group established two retail outlets, the Panmai Store in the Kasetvisai district of Roi Et and the Naraiphan Store in Bangkok.

In addition to its business operations, the Group was concerned with the welfare of its members and their families, and sought to ensure their social stability and safety. It did so by offering health insurance, life in-surance, and education for the members' children. The Group also had a savings system to encourage members' saving and to reduce the Group's reliance on outside capital.

The Panmai Group's operating capital came from a number of sources, including a loan from ATA, capital mobilized from the members, shares held by NGOs (ATA, the Agricultural Reformation and Rural Development Project, and the Royal Property), and profits saved from the Group's busi-ness operations. The Group was able to increase the ratio of shares held by its members from 25 percent in 1991–1992 to 63 percent in 1997. The Group paid out dividends to the member-shareholders at a rate of 10 per-cent annually, in addition to the income they earned by producing goods for the Group.

Two business associations also became involved in supporting the Group: the Agricultural Reformation and Rural Development Project and the Promotion of the Learning Procedure for Rural Development Project.

In addition to providing funds, these organizations helped to improve the efficiency of the housewives network through assisting in the development of business-oriented management skills and in the promotion of leadership skills by expanding the members' understanding of society, culture, and politics.

As the project became successful, the number of community groups involved expanded dramatically. Currently, this project comprises 24 villages in six districts of the provinces of Roi Et, Sisaket, and Surin. By 1991, the membership in the weavers group had already grown to include nearly 500 women from these areas.

In addition, the Panmai Group had broadened its network by working cooperatively with other groups conducting similar activities, such as the Weaving Group of the Northeastern Development Foundation (NETCRAFT) in Surin, the Handicraft Center for Northeastern Women's Development (Prae Pan Group) in Khon Kaen, and the Traditional Material Weaving Group of Waang Noi District. Together these groups formed the Northeastern Handicraft and Women's Development Network (NET), which had the status of a working committee affiliated with the Committee on the Coordination of Nongovernmental Organizations of the Northeastern Region. NET played an important role in the determination of prices and in the establishment of markets through such means as a joint venture in a cloth shop. As a member of NET, Panmai Group became active in addressing a broader range of issues, including political participation, women and resource management, gender issues, alien labor, and community business taxes.

The expansion of the Group's base and network, combined with the skills gained through its traditional handweaving business, increased the group's confidence and enabled it to mobilize external cooperation with partners in development. A prime example was the Group's ability to venture into a new business with Bangchak Petroleum Public Co., Ltd.

COOPERATION WITH BANGCHAK PETROLEUM

Bangchak Petroleum is a primarily state-owned oil company that markets, distributes, and refines crude oil and petroleum products. The products are marketed through company-owned service stations and minimarts. Bangchak is known for being a company that seeks to expand its business activities through cooperation with the community. The company provides community organizations with opportunities to learn to manage and administer business enterprises and to become entrepreneurs in the

future. Sophon Supapongse, the managing director of Bangchak Petroleum, has proposed that ownership of community business should be in
the form of business networks that coordinate activities within a community. In other words, he recommends tying together various individual
activities into business-oriented networks. This concept relies on cooperation between the private business sector, community organizations,
and other parties, such as NGOs and the public sector, in order to promote
integrated community development.

In 1995, the Panmai Group began working with Bangchak to develop
a feasibility plan through the company's existing program. That year, the
Group was able to expand its operations through the investment of 6 million baht (US$163,710) in a gas station venture, known as the Tongkula
Petroleum Company. Shares of this company were sold to more than 900
people from 31 communities, including the Panmai Group (31 percent),
other villagers (28 percent), the general public (6 percent), and developers and NGOs (35 percent). In establishing this venture, ATA had purchased 3 rai of land and prepared the site for Bangchak and the Tongkula
Petroleum Company to rent. Bangchak provided support in the form of
construction and equipment investment for two posts connected to the
oil tanks and four gas pumps. In addition, Bangchak's training division
supported the sales system and management training for the community
organization.

Tongkula Petroleum's sales have increased steadily since 1995. The gas
station is ideally located in a heavily trafficked location, and as a result,
there is strong potential not only for the gas station to succeed but also
for it to venture into other compatible businesses, such as minimarts and
restaurants. Although present figures show a loss, the majority of shares
in the company are still in the hands of the community, and it is anticipated that this business will be a good income generator that will support the operations of the community organization in the future.

The Group's partnership with Bangchak took a second form as well.
As noted above, the handweaving business had expanded to include the
production of ready-to-wear garments. When the Ministry of Industry initiated the Rural Industrialization Project, the Panmai Group took advantage of the opportunity to propose a project in which the Group would
produce uniforms for the gas station staff at the Bangchak gas stations.[2]

2. The Rural Industrialization Project aims to support the community in conducting
businesses. There are a number of assistance schemes, such as interest-free loans and
training, according to demand.

The result was a collaborative effort in which Bangchak provides market support through purchase orders of 3,000 pieces a month, and the Ministry of Industry provides support for training and for the employment of ATA staff to advise the Group. This is a pilot project lasting for three years. At present, this project is in its second year and has already increased the Group's production confidence as a result of the guaranteed market.

CONCLUSION

The Panmai Group has achieved success on a number of fronts. It has had a constructive impact on the community by improving the quality of life of the women and their families, by contributing to community development and community organization, and by enhancing the women's ability to operate businesses. Of particular note was the ability of the Group's activities to empower the women in the community. The administrative and management skills the women have acquired have allowed them to contribute to the development of their villages, and in many cases the leaders of the housewives associated with the Panmai Group have gone on to apply their newly developed skills in the local government. Of course, there have also been cases in which the inability to accept women in leadership roles has led to conflict between the housewives groups and community leaders, demonstrating that impediments do still remain to the development of women's role in society.

These positive outcomes from the work of the Panmai Group were the result of its cooperation with other partners throughout its development. In the beginning, this cooperation was limited to the partnership between the community organization and the ATA staff. Financial, technical, and material support was then provided in the early stages by other private nonprofit organizations, such as the Canadian International Development Agency, the Japanese Support Group for Thai Villages, and other private organizations in Japan. As the Group developed into a community business organization, however, it had to shift its strategy and rely on increased cooperation with other sectors of society, and particularly with the corporate sector. The Group has successfully worked with the government sector, the business sector, and domestic and international NGOs in the expansion of its activities, and although still in the early stages, there have been signs of increased multiparty cooperation. The cooperation between the Ministry of Industry, Bangchak Petroleum, the Panmai Group, and ATA in the project to produce shirts for the Bangchak pump staff is one such example. Based on the experiences of the Panmai Group, a number of lessons can be drawn regarding the current status and future direction of multiparty cooperation.

First, effective partnerships should capitalize on the respective strengths that each party brings to the development process, whether it be capital, knowledge, or management skills. To do so, those strengths must be combined in a genuine partnership. Although multisectoral partnerships in Thailand are still in their formative stage, the present image of the relationship between the various partners is that of one party standing on the outside and observing. Development work is concerned with processes—group formation, network building, and so forth—and as a result, it is important that work be performed jointly and problems be solved together. The creation of these types of partnerships is an ongoing process that will undoubtedly require time, and continuity in the personnel involved in these projects will be critical. In addition, since multiparty cooperation relies on the process of learning through action —from planning to implementation—it is important that the partners periodically take stock of the lessons learned and make appropriate adjustments throughout the work process.

Another important criteria for effective partnerships is that there should be understanding of the conditions under which the community business organizations are operating. For example, the Panmai Group weaving business requires a relatively long production time because the products are handwoven. Moreover, the villagers are only able to weave during certain periods of the year. It is important, therefore, that partners remain flexible, and that they provide opportunities for the organization to continue operations and become self-reliant.

Finally, it is important that the government make efforts to create an environment that is conducive to such partnerships. Legal measures, regulations, tax measures, and various rights that do not facilitate this process should be adjusted or applied flexibly to enable the strengths of various sectors to be fully brought to bear on the promotion of economic and social development.

The Panmai Group experience exemplifies a new current of social thought concerning multiparty cooperation and people-centered development, which is an important change in Thai social development. Success is possible only when there is a focused determination to direct the entire society towards prosperity. This means that the partners in development have to closely examine various aspects of the social and economic strains within Thailand and have a clear understanding about the true factors that are contributing to those problems. Coexistence in society demands that all sectors participate in the development process, and that cooperation be based on mutual concern and on a willingness to learn through the process.

All-China Federation of Industry and Commerce and the Glorious Cause Program

Zhang Ye

I N recent years, China's economy and society have undergone a dramatic and fundamental transformation. While many of the changes are positive, the country is also facing a wide array of new challenges, such as an aging population, unemployment, income disparity, and a deteriorating environment. The Chinese government's shift toward greater decentralization has left it struggling to meet these new demands. As a result, the government has become increasingly aware of and more receptive to the creation of new relationships between government, the corporate sector, nongovernmental organizations (NGOs), and local communities.

One such example is the work of the All-China Federation of Industry and Commerce (ACFIC), which initiated an ambitious project in the mid-1990s to alleviate poverty in the western and central regions of China. This initiative, known as the Glorious Cause, has proven to be a successful model of multisectoral cooperation that meets the diverse objectives of the various parties involved.

EVOLUTION OF THE NONPROFIT
AND NONGOVERNMENTAL SECTOR IN CHINA

A TURNING POINT

In many ways, 1998 was an extraordinary year for China. The Ninth National People's Congress elected a new administration committed to moving the country further in the direction of "a small state and a big society," meaning the government will continue to loosen its control of the markets and society and give citizens an increased role in managing their lives. A top priority for the administration therefore is to drastically downsize governmental agencies and to reform state-owned enterprises. To help ease the Southeast Asian monetary crisis, the new administration also made a strong commitment to maintain the value of China's currency. Fulfilling these commitments simultaneously will not be easy. Structural reform will, at the very least, lead to a significant increase in unemployment and social disruption, and the decision not to devalue the renminbi is expected to hinder China's exports, thus making it difficult to reach the annual target of 8 percent economic growth even under the best of circumstances.

Just as the administration was trying to grapple with these issues, unprecedented flooding hit in the southern and northeastern regions of China, resulting in thousands of deaths and leaving millions of people homeless. Faced with problems on so many fronts, the government felt overwhelmed, and so was slow to react to the crisis. Instead, it was the nonprofit sector that leapt quickly into action, taking the initiative to organize the nation to fight the flooding. Major NGOs in Beijing launched fund-raising campaigns. China Charity Federation, one of the largest NGOs in China, for example, was the first to organize disaster relief activities, and was able to raise Rmb1.7 billion (US$204 million at Rmb1 = US$0.12) from corporations, overseas groups, and the general public in less than a month's time.[1] NGOs played an important role in coordinating the use of funds and organizing the transportation of materials to those in need. At the community level, NGOs and volunteer groups led disaster relief efforts, providing food, clean water, and medicine, building temporary shelters for those displaced by the floods, arranging for children's schooling, and even saving lives.

In short, the NGO sector in China received a great impetus from the tragedy of the 1998 floods. The sector demonstrated strength and vigor in advancing the welfare of the people, and earned much greater recognition among the Chinese public. This is not to imply, however, that an NGO movement appeared overnight—it has been in existence for decades, beginning with China's reform and opening-up in the late 1970s.

A BRIEF HISTORY

After the Chinese Communist Party emerged victorious from the

---

1. *People's Daily*, August 23, 1998.

proletarian revolution in 1949, the Chinese government established a planned economy that was expected to represent the interests of the masses and distribute social wealth equally among the members of society. Citizens' identities were closely bound to their working units, which supervised their behavior and provided a social safety net. The socialist notion of the relationship between state and citizen allowed little room for nongovernmental organizations to exist. At the same time, public ownership allowed the government to monopolize resources, leaving NGOs with little access to financial or other means of support. This, combined with the fact that Chinese laws and regulations concentrated on the punishment of counter-revolutionaries, fostered a social environment that was quite unfavorable to organizing citizens' groups outside of the governmental structure, making the creation of independent NGOs impossible.

The policy of reform and opening-up initiated toward the end of the 1970s brought about great changes. In the economic field, the traditional centralized planned economy was gradually replaced by a socialist market economy. In the early 1980s, the state's direct control of the economy declined and, conversely, non-state enterprises grew rapidly, soon comprising the majority of China's economy. Along with the decentralization process, however, came an erosion of the central government's ability to meet societal needs. The government can no longer provide the kind of social safety net to the public that it once did. Social problems such as care for the elderly, children, and the handicapped, relief for the poor and unemployed, and management of the environment all require attention and resources that exceed the capacity of the central government. Under such circumstances, it has become increasingly understood and accepted that certain things cannot and should not be handled by the government, and must instead be taken care of by the people themselves.

These changes have been accompanied by significant legal reform. Chinese society has gradually changed from rule by men to rule by law. In recent years, hundreds of laws have been passed by the National People's Congress, many of which are specifically intended to restrain the government's abuse of power and to protect citizens' rights. The Administrative Litigation Law passed in 1991, for example, allowed citizens to sue the government for the first time in China's history, while the Criminal Procedure Law, passed in 1996, introduced the principle of presumption of innocence. This improved legal environment has encouraged the involvement of citizens in China's social and economic life.

China also promulgated in 1998 a new Regulation on the Registration and Management of Social Organizations, and Interim Provisions on the Management and Registration of Nongovernmental and Nonprofit Organizations. Although the impact of these regulations on the development of NGOs is yet to be tested, they reflect a widely felt need to regulate the existing large variety of NGOs, while at the same time providing guidelines for the future development of the nongovernmental sector. While the new regulations still emphasize control, they also represent the first serious efforts to address the legal status of the emerging NGOs and to establish processes through which the government and NGOs can deal with one another. In this respect, the promulgation of these new regulations should be viewed as progress.

The financial base of NGOs has also expanded in recent years. With the rapid development of the market economy, private entrepreneurs have begun to use their wealth to engage in charitable giving or to sponsor popular cultural activities. Their financial support has made possible the burgeoning of some categories of NGOs that could not otherwise have been established. Overseas Chinese also provide substantial funds for mainland China's charitable activities. A third important source of funds is the foreign community. Foreign foundations and government agencies play an important role in supporting NGOs and in helping create a positive legal environment and management infrastructure.

It may be a common impression that the development of the nonprofit sector is primarily a function of urbanization and democratization. However, in China, the emergence of NGOs and greater citizen participation has also been a rural phenomenon tied to the recollectivization trend that began in the 1980s. The household responsibility system introduced in the late 1970s and early 1980s abolished the old collective system, and while individual household farming still continues, from the mid-1980s many farmers began to realize that the new market economy was rewarding economies of scale to the detriment of individual peasants. They soon felt the need for some kind of organizational structure to cope with their common concerns and, as a result, started to organize themselves into cooperatives, special service teams, or networks of households structured around economic development programs. While this recollectivization process received the endorsement of local governments, it was nonetheless a self-managed movement. These NGOs, which were motivated by economic need, eventually became involved in other social and political activities as well. The village committee elections of the late 1980s and early 1990s were one example of such a bottom-up initiative that in turn had a tremendous impact on the democratic process and further fostered a positive environment for NGO development in rural areas.

It is against this background that Chinese NGOs have been evolving. Currently, nearly 200,000 NGOs have registered with the Ministry of Civil Affairs or at local civil affairs departments. Most NGOs at this time are independent of governmental agencies in terms of their finances. Their funding comes mainly from private donations and sometimes from small businesses that they conduct. As China moves toward "a small state and a big society," the government is expected to become more relaxed and open in its management of the NGO sector. Although they will still have to work within the constraints of China's political structure, Chinese NGOs are expected to become more independent and to shoulder an increasing share of social responsibilities.

EMERGENCE OF THE PRIVATE SECTOR
AND CORPORATE SOCIAL RESPONSIBILITY ACTIVITIES

Another new phenomenon that arose from the 1998 floods was that private corporations began to play an important role in disaster relief. The ACFIC, an organization representing China's private corporations, called upon its members to contribute to the disaster relief campaign, and was quickly able to raise several billion renminbi. Unlike previous disaster relief efforts that relied more heavily on overseas Chinese and foreign organizations, this time indigenous groups provided the major resources, accounting for 60 percent of the total donations for flood relief.

China's private sector itself is a new phenomenon derived from China's reform and opening-up process. Before 1949, national industry in China was almost nonexistent, and the economy was dominated by the so-called bureaucratic capitalists of the four big Kuomintang families. Corruption, compounded by constant wars and natural disasters, severely weakened China's small and vulnerable industry, and on the eve of the founding of the new China, the country's economy was on the verge of collapse.

After the People's Republic of China was established in 1949, the Communist Party did away with the semifeudal economy, together with the old political system and cultural traditions. In its place came a national industrial economy and a collective agricultural economy with public ownership—i.e., ownership by the state—as the core principle. Within a short period of time, the Chinese Communist Party took over Rmb15 billion (US$1.8 billion) worth of assets from the "bureaucratic capitalists" and began to transform the economy by merging private enterprises with publicly owned corporations. By the end of 1956, 82 percent of China's 2.4 million private enterprises had been transformed into state-owned enterprises. The Great Leap Forward in the late 1950s, which aimed at achieving communism, further reduced non-state ownership and inflicted still greater damage to China's economy, while the Cultural Revolution in the 1960s and 1970s not only abolished all non-state ownership but also attacked all vestiges of the old "capitalism, feudalism, and imperialism." Former "capitalists" were accused of being "class enemies" and were purged. This situation persisted until the end of the 1970s, when China launched its reform program.

The reforms first focused on rural areas, introducing a "household responsibility system," which allowed a market economy to emerge in the countryside.[2] Township-and-village enterprises (TVEs), characterized by their non-state nature, soon altered the industrial mix.[3] Urban reforms followed in the middle of the 1980s, first with the withdrawal of government from many enterprises, and then with new measures to encourage the establishment of more private and non-state corporations. Today, private enterprises account for more than 60 percent of the economy and are playing an essential role in China's economic and social spheres.

As private enterprises became more profitable they also became more involved in social and cultural activities. In the early stages, private enterprises were more interested in supporting cultural and sports activities from which they could easily receive publicity that would benefit their market image. More recently, however, an increasing number of companies have become aware of their social responsibilities, and have begun contributing to such causes as the environment, poverty alleviation, education, and welfare. In part, this may reflect a desire for positive social

2. The household responsibility system introduced at the end of the 1970s replaced the commune system that had emphasized a planned and collective economy. Under the new household responsibility system, land was divided among individual households, which in turn had freedom and autonomy in farm production. Once the agricultural quota set by the state had been fulfilled, the households were free to conduct other businesses.

3. TVEs started to develop in the late 1970s and early 1980s. They are small enterprises, usually owned by the township or village, with shares held by individuals or households and groups.

recognition and increased respect, but it also reflects an understanding that only by investing in social development and being engaged in social change can an enterprise benefit in the long run.

ALL-CHINA FEDERATION
OF INDUSTRY AND COMMERCE

The ACFIC is an organization that has experienced firsthand the fluctuations of contemporary Chinese history. The ACFIC was first established in 1952 by a group of private industrialists who represented patriotic nationalists and supported the Chinese Communist Party's initiative of transforming the capitalist economy into one of socialism. The Party recognized those private businesspeople as among "the exploited mass organizations, democratic parties, minority nationalities, overseas Chinese and other patriots who should be united with the Communist Party to form a united front against Chiang Kai-shek's regime and who should contribute to the establishment of a democratic united government."[4] In fact, in the early days of the People's Republic of China, leading members of the ACFIC became renowned figures in the United Front and Political Consultative Conference. During the Cultural Revolution of the 1960s and 1970s, however, all private entrepreneurs were purged. The leaders of the ACFIC were sent to the countryside for rehabilitation, and the ACFIC was forced to close down; it was unable to function for more than ten years.

Not until late 1979, when China launched its reform and opening-up policy, did the ACFIC reappear. In October 1979, the Fourth Congress of the ACFIC was held, during which its members recommitted themselves to making the ACFIC "a contributor to China's Four Modernizations drive."[5] Over the ensuing two decades, the ACFIC has coordinated the work of collective and private enterprises. Many of its members were pioneers in running China's TVEs, and the ACFIC draws on their experience to provide economic and business consulting to its members and other corporations. It also uses its network to facilitate the mainland's economic interaction with Taiwan, Hong Kong, and other overseas Chinese.

4. "Manifesto of the Chinese People's Liberation Army," October 15, 1947, in *The Selected Works of Mao Zedong (Vol. 4)*, p. 1237.

5. The "Four Modernizations" refers to the goal of Chinese domestic policy, as announced in 1978, to modernize China in four specific areas: agriculture, industry, national defense, and science and technology.

THE GLORIOUS CAUSE

In the past few years, ACFIC members have broadened their focus to include political and social issues. One issue that has captured the attention and commitment of the private entrepreneurs is China's poverty. As of 1993, China still had 80 million people living in poverty.[6] While the reform process has benefited millions of people in urban and rural areas of China, millions more in the country's remote areas have not been able to benefit because of poor transportation and communication infrastructure, inadequate natural resources, or other reasons. The policy of letting some people get rich first has created a gaping disparity between the rich and poor.

The State Council in 1993 launched a poverty alleviation campaign aimed at getting those 80 million people out of poverty before the end of the century. To do so, however, the government realized that it needed a new strategy. Since the 1950s, the government had poured millions of yuan into relief funds to assist the poor in meeting basic needs. While this alleviated the immediate problem, it did not address the underlying causes of poverty. Accordingly, the government's new strategy aimed at establishing a sustainable socioeconomic system based on a market economy. Recognizing that it could not manage a task of this proportion alone, the government called on the whole nation to respond.

As a result, at an April 1994 meeting of the ACFIC, ten private entrepreneurs led by Liu Yonghao initiated the Glorious Cause, which urged all ACFIC members and other private businesspeople to join in the effort to assist the poorer regions of the country. The Glorious Cause, as Liu put it, "was based on simple goodwill—those who benefited from China's economic reform and got rich first shall return some of their gains to the society, and particularly to the poor areas where people still don't have enough food and clothes."[7]

Their initiative received a positive response from many private businesspeople. As China's market economy is still in its infancy, most businesses are still small, community-based corporations, and many have their roots in the TVEs, having started as collective enterprises in rural

6. Poverty is defined as having an annual income less than Rmb530 (US$63.60).

7. "Review of the Work of the Glorious Cause for the Past Year," a speech by Liu Yonghao given at the Fourth Panel of the Standing Committee of the Seventh Congress of the All-China Federation of Industry and Commerce, in *Glorious Cause Journal*, vol. 10, May 15, 1995.

areas. Accordingly, private entrepreneurs often feel indebted to the communities and welcomed a chance to give something back. Since the start of the Glorious Cause in 1994, over 2,000 private entrepreneurs have participated in the program. So far, they have implemented 3,000 projects with investments of Rmb52 billion (US$6.24 billion) as seed money and donated funds of Rmb400 million (US$48 million). They have provided technical, managerial, and sales training to 40,000 people, and have helped 550,000 people to escape from poverty.[8]

As more people became involved in the Glorious Cause, an organization was needed to coordinate its work. Accordingly, in late 1994, the Council for the Promotion of the Glorious Cause was established, headquartered in ACFIC. Over the next four years, the Council set up more than 30 branch offices throughout China. The activities of the Council include providing information, organizing survey research in the poor regions, coordinating with the local government and NGOs, and handling public relations for the Glorious Cause participants.

CHARACTERISTICS OF THE GLORIOUS CAUSE

The first question facing those who initiated the Glorious Cause was how best to contribute to the economic development of impoverished areas while at the same time helping the investors to benefit. Past experiences had clearly demonstrated that a long-term, sustainable development system based on a market economy was needed to alleviate poverty in these regions. To establish such a system, however, required the building of infrastructure, the training of personnel, and the establishment of links with domestic and international markets. Accordingly, these tasks became the initial focus of the Glorious Cause's development strategies.

The second question that needed to be answered was where to invest. While two-thirds of China's territory is considered to be poor, 70 percent of those living in poverty are located in the central and western parts of China. These areas also have more natural resources and have been less developed to date, offering a promising market for businesses to target. The needs of the region thus coincided well with the market potential, which is precisely the type of convergence of interests that the Glorious Cause was seeking. As explained by Hu Deping, vice chairman of ACFIC,

8. Work Report of the First Board Meeting of the China Council for the Promotion of the Glorious Cause, as published in the "Collection of Materials of the First Board of the China Council for the Promotion of the Glorious Cause," December 1996.

the Glorious Cause represents the "socialist concept of public interest combined with corporate profit."[9]

CORPORATE-COMMUNITY PARTNERSHIP

Decisions on the Glorious Cause projects are made by the corporations. Since most of China's private enterprises are still small, the managers and board members play an essential role in the decision-making process. Implementation of the Glorious Cause projects is a joint effort between the investors, local governments, and NGOs. In most cases, the corporate investors provide funding, technical assistance, and materials. Employees often become involved as project coordinators and technical advisors. Local organizations offer labor, land, and sometimes matching funds. Depending on the situation, Glorious Cause initiators might choose to work with agricultural cooperatives; with the local government, which would then contract the work out to village committees; or with local agricultural companies that in turn would contract out to local households. The following cases illustrate the types of projects that the Glorious Cause implements.

CASE ONE   Liu Yonghao, one of the initiators of the Glorious Cause, is chairman of the board of the New Hope Agriculture Corporation. He was listed by *Forbes* in 1994 and 1995 as the top private entrepreneur in China. Once a poor peasant, Liu benefited from China's reform policy and became a wealthy entrepreneur. In 1994, while participating in a survey tour of several poor provinces, he was deeply struck by China's poverty and became an advocate for corporate action, challenging his fellow ACFIC members to join him in responding to the problem.

He then picked some of the poorest sites in China, such as the Yi Autonomous Prefecture of Sichuan Province and the Da Bieshan region of Henan Province, as the focus for his efforts. Contracts for fodder plants were signed between the New Hope Agricultural Corporation and the local county governments, but the project was contracted out to village committees, agricultural cooperatives, local private enterprises, and to networks of households. The New Hope Corporation invested Rmb47.76 million (US$5.73 million) to build dozens of fodder plants. The corporation designed and provided the materials for the plants, while the local organizations coordinated the labor force. Once the plants were completed,

9. Ibid.

job priority was given to poor local households. Technical personnel designed by the New Hope Agricultural Corporation extended their services, and local organizations coordinated the training at the grass-roots level. Thanks to the successful collaboration among these groups, the household income in these areas increased dramatically in just two years.

CASE TWO   Another private entrepreneur, Zhang Zhiting, the general manager of a pharmaceutical company, chose Guizhou Province, another of the poorest provinces, as the site for a Glorious Cause project. Guizhou is primarily an agricultural province, but because of poor soil and limited irrigated land, grain production has not even met the province's own consumption needs. Agriculture also does not generate sufficient income for the local people, so the ethnic minorities in the townships where Zhang chose to invest have lived by collecting firewood or picking wild plants. Their per capita annual income was about Rmb100 (US$12). Lack of funding, technology, and skills were formidable constraints on the income-generating ability of the people. Zhang's goal was therefore to introduce more effective methods of animal husbandry and agriculture. While these projects could bring income to the local peasants, the products could also eventually bring his enterprise some profit as well.

Zhang identified two townships in Guizhou and signed an agreement with the two township governments by which he was to invest Rmb470,000 (US$56,400) for the purchase of black goats and seeds for Chinese herbal medicines. The goats and herbs were then raised and managed by local households. Zhang formulated a revolving poverty alleviation project, allowing those who are successful in raising the black goats to keep their income. Instead of paying the company back for the original goats, they are obligated to give the same number of goats to other poor households. In this way, the project has a multiplier effect, allowing an increasing number of households to escape from poverty. After two years of work, 300–400 peasants had participated in the project, and the townships' annual per capita income had reached Rmb3,000 (US$360)—a thirtyfold increase.

CASE THREE   Shenzhen Haishang Corporation chose Inner Mongolia as the focus of its project. Inner Mongolia is underdeveloped at the moment, but it has great potential as a market economy and should be capable of attracting investors once a channel is established. Shenzhen

Haishang decided to turn the old deserted streets in Hohhot, the capital of Inner Mongolia, into a commercial center. To do so, the corporation signed an agreement with the local government, which in turn subcontracted work to local private companies. Together, they cleaned up the old streets and built a low-price market. The corporation also helped link the market with the central and western regions of China. Agricultural products have started to flow across the borders, giving new life to the economy of these poor regions. Shenzhen Haishang has invested Rmb22 million (US$2.64 million) in these projects and has provided hundreds of jobs.

These cases are just a sample of the work that the Glorious Cause has done to date. Other types of projects include:

- agricultural development, including reclaiming waste land, conducting animal husbandry, and improving agricultural productivity;
- natural resource exploitation, including building mineral and metallurgical factories and coal mines;
- industrial and agricultural processing, such as the processing of herbal medicine and other agricultural products;
- labor migration, including organizing workers from poor regions to work in the more developed areas and encouraging the migration of poor villages to better places;
- personnel training, including training in technical and management skills; and
- donations for such projects as the building of local schools, improving access to drinking water, and so on.

All of these projects have been completed through partnerships with the local communities.

CONCLUSION

When summarizing the accomplishments of the Glorious Cause, Hu points to four major achievements. First, the Glorious Cause has mobilized and coordinated private enterprises to contribute to the national need for poverty alleviation. Second, it has built a bridge between those who got rich first and those who have lagged behind, helping the wealthy businesspeople to translate their goodwill into effective practices. Third, the Glorious Cause has initiated a new and more effective method of poverty alleviation, to replace the stopgap measures of the past. And fourth, it has helped local communities to develop new approaches to economic development.

For these reasons, the Glorious Cause has won broad recognition throughout Chinese society and is regarded as a pioneering initiative that links various social forces for a common cause. The efforts of these corporations have clearly been appreciated by the communities where the work has been implemented. As more communities benefit from the Glorious Cause, and as the media continues to give a good deal of publicity to the projects, word has spread to other parts of the country. An increasing number of townships, villages, and local NGOs have begun to call on the offices of the All-China Council for the Promotion of Glorious Cause for collaboration. In turn, the Council has become even more active in mobilizing its members to participate in the Glorious Cause.

The projects have also won the appreciation and respect of the government. In 1996, the United Front Work Department of the Chinese Communist Party Central Committee and the State Council's Leading Group for Economic Development in the Poor Areas issued a circular to local government departments calling on them to support the Glorious Cause's economic development projects. President Jiang Zemin has spoken highly of the Glorious Cause, noting that "it carries on Chinese traditional ethics [and] promotes mutual prosperity."[10]

As China struggles to manage the dramatic shifts that are occurring in its society, institutional and organizational innovation have become necessities. The challenge ahead is to find new methods of interaction between government, corporations, and NGOs that will meet the respective interests and objectives of each actor while serving the public good. The Glorious Cause offers one successful model of such a partnership, demonstrating a novel approach that links the interests of the country, the enterprises, the NGOs, and the communities. Moreover, it is a good example of the contributions that corporations can make to the development of civil society.

10. President Jiang Zemin's endorsement of the Glorious Cause on April 16, 1996, as published in *China Industry and Commerce*, vol. 4, 1997.

5 Cebu Hillyland Development Program

Cristina V. Pavia

IN late 1987, the city of Cebu in central Philippines was booming. Sunny, pleasant Cebu was no longer just a popular tourist destination for scuba divers and beach lovers. Local and foreign investors were establishing new businesses in the city, and the industrial sector was quickly expanding. Standing in the way of further development, however, were two serious constraints: limited land for commercial and industrial use owing to the mountainous terrain, and a water supply shortage.

The source of the city's water was in the watersheds of the uplands, a resource that was in critical condition as a result of years of deforestation and neglect. Communities living in the area of the watersheds were among the poorest of Cebu's populace. Clearing farm plots and gathering firewood were their primary means of generating income, both of which contributed to environmental damage. Business leaders thought that by providing them with an alternative livelihood and encouraging them to plant trees, these communities could become responsible caretakers of the watersheds. Cebu's continued prosperity depended on restoring the productive capacity of its uplands. To achieve this goal, a multisectoral effort was launched, bringing together the resources of government, business, and nongovernmental organizations (NGOs) to work with the upland communities for the promotion of social development and environmental protection.

BACKGROUND

Metropolitan Cebu enjoyed a central, strategic location in the Philippines as a gateway for trade. The port was the country's busiest, accounting for 80 percent of interisland shipping and servicing direct routes to Taiwan, Japan, Hong Kong, and South Korea. Cebu also had the country's fastest growing economy, boosted in the early 1980s by the metropolitan government's successful "Ce-boom! Ce-boom!" campaign, which attracted both tourists and foreign investors. Trade and manufacturing grew briskly with the establishment of economic hubs such as the Mactan Export Processing Zone, and Cebu's tourist industry also thrived, capturing one-third of all foreign visitors to the country.

Cebu's continued urbanization, however, was hindered by the lack of flatlands for commercial expansion. Cebu's predominantly mountainous interior took up 78 percent of its total area, leaving the city and its 1.5 million people crowded into the remaining 7,000 hectares of flatlands. As a result, the government and private developers sought to expand into the uplands or to reclaim coastal waters.

The second issue was the growing shortage of water. By 1988, the government-owned Metro Cebu Water District (MCWD) was supplying only 55 percent of Cebu's total water needs. Areas without MCWD service resorted to digging private deep wells. This pervasive practice had resulted in salt intrusion in the aquifers. To keep Cebu's growth on track, the government needed to better manage existing water sources even as it developed new sources of water.

The city was supplied by three central watersheds in the hillyland. These watersheds were open grasslands located on the steep upland slopes. Cebu's forests had mostly been lost to cultivation by early human settlements, and the remaining forest growth provided barely 7 percent forest cover. Of the three watersheds, the Mananga Watershed was Metro Cebu's major water source, covering some 8,000 hectares of catchment area. With 88 percent of its total area eroded, however, the government declared in 1989 that Mananga was in critical condition.

Seventeen of the city's *barangay* (the basic sociopolitical unit in the Philippines) were located in Mananga, comprising 4,000 households. As was true in much of the uplands, these were households of poor farmers who tilled plots of about one-third hectare. The land was dry, hard, and prone to rainfall run-off and soil erosion, and over the years the farms had become less and less productive. The few ears of corn, bell peppers, and tomatoes that were harvested were small and of low quality. Farmers kept the corn for food and sold the tomatoes and bell peppers on the city outskirts for a meager amount of cash. Some farmers also sold firewood and charcoal to augment their earnings. The farmers earned an average net income of P850 (US$212.50 at P1 = US$0.25) per month—well below the poverty line of P3,000 (US$750).

THE CEBU HILLYLAND DEVELOPMENT PROGRAM

In 1988, the city government of Cebu, with help from the World Bank, launched a new program to develop and reforest the hillyland. To involve the private sector and the upland villages, a meeting was called by Mayor Tomas Osmeña at the City Hall. In attendance were village leaders from 20 upland communities, officials from various government agencies, and representatives of businesses and NGOs. The mayor invited each organization to take the lead in the development of certain upland villages by way of "adopting" them and seeing to it that the needed resources were provided. The Department of Agriculture took responsibility for eight villages in the central hillyland section, and three villages in the southwestern section were selected by an NGO, the Philippine Business for Social Progress (PBSP). Other NGOs declined to adopt villages but pledged livelihood and technology support. The city government was left with 19 villages to adopt.

INVOLVEMENT OF THE PHILIPPINE BUSINESS FOR SOCIAL PROGRESS

Following the meeting, Mayor Osmeña met with the PBSP Board based in Cebu to firm up the NGO's participation in the program. PBSP is a well-established nonprofit social development organization with a history of corporate involvement in poverty alleviation programs. It is the Philippines' largest grant-making and operating foundation, with offices in the three major regions of the country and a professional staff of 166 in 1989. Its Board of Trustees is composed of chief executive officers and presidents of some of the biggest corporations in the country. Over the years, the Board has established a close relationship with the professional staff, bringing an effective combination of business discipline and social development skills to the implementation of projects. PBSP also has a network of 500 NGO partners that assist in conducting programs.

PBSP was organized by the business community in Manila in 1970 as an expression of corporate social responsibility. PBSP's member companies contribute a percentage of their annual net income for its projects. Beyond writing out checks, however, the corporate representatives are encouraged to become directly involved in various PBSP projects. These projects deal with micro and small business management, appropriate agricultural technologies, community organizing, institution building, and environmental protection.

In 1988, the foundation was supported by 119 companies, 13 of which were based in the Visayas region where Cebu is located. The PBSP office in Cebu City had just been opened that year to service the Visayas-based member companies and to implement more responsive programs in that region. Its operations, run by a staff of 20, were directed by a local Board. The first chair, Erramon Aboitiz, represented the Aboitiz Group of Companies, Cebu's largest and oldest shipping enterprise. Aboitiz had been serving on the national PBSP Board, which provided the institutional policies and directions of the programs; the local Board in Cebu directed the implementation of those programs.

Mayor Osmeña approached PBSP, hoping that it would be able to tap the resources of the business community on behalf of the Hillyland Development Program. He also recognized PBSP as an effective development organization and asked that it apply its community organizing skills with the farmers.[1] As it turned out, the mayor's timing could not have been better. The local Board was looking to launch a potentially high-impact, high-visibility program to involve member companies. As Aboitiz explained, "We needed to get the local business community involved or interested in PBSP and social development. The hillylands project of the city government was the impact program we were looking for. I personally thought that business and government could do a lot together, as partners in development."[2]

The Board listened to the mayor as he traced the city's worsening problems to the conditions in the uplands. The water shortages and the flooding that occurred in some parts of the city when it rained were the

1. The foundation had earned a reputation for developing new and effective antipoverty programs. Recognizing this, the newly installed government of Corazon Aquino, seeking broad sectoral participation in the task of nation building, had contracted out to PBSP its major poverty alleviation programs in Samar and Negros, provinces in the same region as Cebu.

2. Interview with Erramon Aboitiz, April 3, 1998, Cebu City.

effects of a deteriorated watershed, explained the mayor. In addition, mendicancy in the city was growing as poor people from the uplands were coming to the city to try to eke out a living. The government was proposing reforestation and community development as a solution.

The Board pledged its support for the three villages of Sinsin, Sudlon I, and Sudlon II, located in the southwestern section of Cebu in the Mananga reserve. It then instructed the professional staff to undertake a survey of the villages and to propose how to conduct a reforestation program. Mayor Osmeña promised to improve the roads, provide electric power in the project area, and lend technical assistance.

In February 1989, the local PBSP Board and the staff joined Mayor Osmeña in their first trip to the three upland villages. It was 30 kilometers from the city over rough roads. The visitors took in the view from the hillyland—a bare landscape dotted by some farms. In front of the gathered members of the community, Mayor Osmeña introduced PBSP and talked about a reforestation program. The response, however, echoed the initial findings of the PBSP staff's survey: The people in these communities had more immediate needs than planting trees. They wanted to be able to send their children to schools close to home, to have better access to a doctor when they were sick, and to earn higher incomes.

Consequently, the Board approved a program that was directly responsive to the community's immediate needs for potable water, health services, community schools, and livelihood opportunities. Reforestation was put off as an immediate activity, although it was kept as the larger goal. The staff developed an initial four-pronged program that aimed at:

- strengthening the existing community organization and increasing its farmer-members;
- addressing basic socioeconomic needs, including financial assistance for livelihood projects;
- demonstrating technologies to make farm plots more productive; and
- building awareness about the watershed environment.

PBSP committed to support the Cebu Hillyland Development Program from 1989 to 1996, to assist 582 upland families overcome poverty and participate in watershed protection. The program was based on an initial partnership between business and government, with PBSP serving to facilitate the process. Eventually, when community organizations in the three villages had developed, PBSP drew them into the partnership as well.

SHAPING A PARTNERSHIP FOR THE ENVIRONMENT

PHASE I (1989–1992): FUND RAISING AND
MOBILIZING RESOURCES FOR THE UPLANDS

PBSP launched the program in May 1989, at the exclusive Casino Español de Cebu. In attendance were representatives from member companies and other companies based in Cebu. The national PBSP Board was represented by Chair Andres Soriano III, then chief executive officer of San Miguel Corporation. The secretary of the Department of Environment and Natural Resources and Mayor Osmeña were keynote speakers, both stressing that it was a race against time to rehabilitate the Mananga watershed. As the event closed, company representatives signed a statement of interest to participate in the PBSP program.

Getting business participation was difficult at first, according to Aboitiz. "People basically don't want to be pioneering. They want to know that it is successful first, and then to latch on to the success. So it was important that PBSP member companies kick start it. After that, it was easier to get people in."[3] Accordingly, the Board set an example by getting personally involved. One Board member brought water drillers to the three villages for the deep well projects; a second member sent engineers to look into the construction of water systems to irrigate the farms; and yet another engaged technical personnel to conduct water mapping of the area.

The staff prepared brochures and a video presentation about the urgency of the problem in the uplands and circulated these to the business community. The Board also stepped up its campaign from one-on-one lunches with colleagues to organized meetings with the chambers of commerce. It asked for human, financial, and technical resources from companies to install potable water systems, build catchment areas and impounding systems for upland farms irrigation, send out medical missions, construct health centers, and procure seedlings for reforestation. The campaign also tapped medical associations, such as the Cebu Doctor's Hospital, which agreed to hold a total of 15 regular clinics in the uplands. The Kauswagan Foundation, which was accredited by the city health department, set up a community drug store. Schools and their student organizations held citywide poster-making contests about the watershed environment. Company technicians and government agencies

3. Ibid.

contributed technical know-how in constructing springboxes and hand pumps to provide drinking water to the three villages. For the reforestation efforts, companies donated seeds, seedlings, farm implements, and trucking services. From 1989 to 1993, PBSP raised ₱3.4 million (US$850,000) for the program and received donations of in-kind goods and services worth more than ₱200,000 (US$50,000).

FUND RAISING BY THE HILLYLAND COMMITTEE   As the program developed into a major undertaking, the Board set up a four-person Hillyland Committee to oversee the program. The committee developed three successful strategies to further involve the business sector: the Adopt-a-Hectare Campaign, the Reforestation Caravan, and the Hillyland Christmas Card Project.

The Adopt-a-Hectare scheme, started in 1990, allowed corporate donors to take up the cost of reforestation of a full hectare at roughly ₱21,000 (US$5,250). As noted by Leo Hilado, then the PBSP operations manager in the Visayas region, "The scheme gave a clear address of their financial help, which they liked. It was very successful in terms of raising awareness and funds."[4] More than 60 companies participated in the campaign, which continued until 1996 and contributed a total of ₱977,400 (US$244,350) for reforestation.

The Reforestation Caravan involved companies in a weekend tree-planting excursion to the three villages. Some companies had donated to Adopt-a-Hectare and subsequently encouraged their employees to plant the trees in the company's hectare. Before each group set out from downtown Cebu, a government official spoke to the volunteers about the reforestation program and the collaboration with PBSP. In the uplands, the visitors were introduced to the community leaders and to the claimant of the area, who would care for the trees. Members of the community prepared the seedlings and the holes in the ground for the visitors, and set up proper markers bearing the names of the companies. After planting the seedlings, everyone shared a snack, sometimes including the local delicacy of lechon, or roast pork. The mood was festive, and the gathering gave the employees an opportunity to interact with the farmers.

PBSP organized an average of three to five caravans a year. At times, as many as 100 corporate employees from various companies would participate, spending the greater part of the day in the uplands. The companies

4. Interview with Leo Hildado, August 1998, Center for Rural Technology Development, Laguna.

covered the costs for the trips, PBSP paid for the seedlings from donations, and the farmers contributed their time.

In 1991, the Board launched the Hillyland Christmas Card Project, a
campaign to increase awareness about environmental issues. Every
year, school children participated in a drawing contest that was judged
by people from the business community. The winning entries were fea-
tured on Christmas cards which included a return slip that allowed the
recipient of the card to have a tree planted in his or her name. The cost
of the card included PBSP's cost for planting one tree. From 1991 to
1996, the project succeeded in selling 57,500 cards, bringing in ₱865,000
(US$216,250) to the reforestation effort. The cards themselves, as well as
media coverage of the project in both the Cebu and Manila dailies, served
to heighten awareness of the issue and publicize the PBSP program.

MOBILIZING COMMUNITY RESOURCES   As the promotions and fund-
raising campaign went on in the city's lowlands, PBSP started the community organizing work in the three upland villages. The PBSP team, made
up of one program manager, one technical officer, and a professional community organizer, immersed themselves in village life. Building up the existing farmers' organizations was a long process, but by 1991 there were
three organizations that had formally registered with the appropriate government agencies.[5] Rodrigo Lachica, the first PBSP field manager, remem-
bered the many challenges that they had to overcome, such as apathy and
the suspicion of PBSP having a communist ideology. But the most difficult obstacle to overcome was the communities' skepticism about PBSP's
interest in them. "We had to gain their trust. We talked about what PBSP
had done in other upland areas; also we explained that no company had
any self-interest in their area. In time, what convinced them was what
they saw in the demonstration farms that we set up."[6]

DEMONSTRATION FARMS   Two demonstration farms were set up in each
of the three villages. One was a PBSP farm and the other was a community

5. The three organizations were the Sudlon I Multi-Purpose Cooperative, with 112 members, the Sudlon II Farmers Livelihood and Training Service Foundation (SUFALTRAS),
with 204 members, and the Sinsin Multi-Purpose Cooperative, with 98 members. While
SUFALTRAS, being a foundation, differed from the other two cooperatives in terms of
nature of organization, the conduct of their activities was similar. Thus, for the purposes of this chapter, the three organizations are referred to as "cooperatives."

6. Interview with Rodrigo Lachica, July 1998, Quezon City.

farm owned by the *barangay* leader. The PBSP farms demonstrated land contouring, or multistory farming, to stem soil erosion. PBSP also conducted a market survey as the basis for technology testing and dissemination of crops such as lettuce and cabbage. The cooperative farm replicated the PBSP farm, using the help of some 30 to 50 farmers from the community. Farmers were willing to try new crops as soon as they realized that they would fetch higher prices. In time, farmers were also introduced to integrated pest management, composting, and other crop diversification technologies. PBSP's coaching was reinforced by training from the field officers of government agencies. By 1991, the majority of the farmers were using new technologies in their farms. The farmer who best implemented these new techniques became PBSP's "Hillyland Farmer of the Year" and received a prize from member companies or private individuals.

PHASE II (1992–1994): TECHNICAL AND MANAGERIAL HELP FOR COMMUNITY ENTERPRISES

REFORESTATION   By early 1993, four years into the program, the three upland villages had hosted close to 580 volunteers from companies, schools, parishes, and civic groups, who had planted trees in their area. They were now able to obtain water for their farms from catchment areas and impounding systems that PBSP had helped to install. They willingly took care of the seedlings and the nurseries, and formed forest patrols to guard the young trees against firewood gatherers. All of the farmers belonging to the three organizations assisted by PBSP stopped chopping wood as a way of augmenting earnings. In addition, to further hasten the planting of trees, PBSP decided to tie production loans to the reforestation activity. This significantly improved the pace of the work, helping to reforest more than 420 hectares by 1996. This increased the forest cover to 22 percent, as compared to 7 percent when the program began.

FARM PRODUCTION AND MARKETING   PBSP provided production loans to the farmers to grow vegetables and mangoes and to raise livestock and poultry. The loans carried an annual interest rate of 18 percent (market rates were at 24 percent at the time). Farmers qualified as borrowers on the basis of their active participation in the cooperative and their continued practice of the sloping agricultural land technology. By 1993, at least 300 farmers had contoured 181 hectares of land.

PBSP had secured the loan fund from its member companies and from foreign donors like MISEREOR of Germany and Trickle Up of New York. The loan fund totaled more than P2 million (US$500,000) in 1992, and loans were made available by PBSP to the cooperatives, which in turn lent them to their members. PBSP also taught the cooperatives to increase their resources through a capital build-up scheme using members' loan repayments. Problems began to arise, however, when unstable markets and damaging effects of typhoons left members unable to repay the loans. In response, PBSP staff first clarified the situation with the communities, explaining that the loans were the primary responsibility of their co-operatives, for which they as members would ultimately pay out of their deposits. But first, the farmers and PBSP had to work together to find solutions to the problem.

Two possible solutions were identified: The first was to help the co-operatives find income-generating projects, and the second was to establish a marketing outlet for the cooperatives that would enable them to collect farm produce as payment from members instead of cash. The marketing outlets were negotiated by PBSP with member companies such as First Philippine Holding Corporation Agri-Division for tomatoes and San Miguel Corporation for a variety of vegetables. The Board approached its business contacts at hotels and restaurants and was able to seal agreements with the Cebu Plaza Hotel, Montebello Hotel, Wendy's restaurant chain, Profoods and Ball's Processing, and Ayala Center. The city government, for its part, provided the upland cooperatives with a stall in the city's main market. On "Tabo," or market day, the farmers were able to double their profits from broccoli, cauliflower, celery, cabbage, lettuce, and tomatoes. The staff gradually worked on the marketing skills of the farmers to enable them to make arrangements themselves, and assisted the cooperatives in upgrading their bookkeeping and project management skills to match their new level of enterprise.

By 1994, 462 households that had been assisted reported earning from P2,000 to P8,500 (US$500 to US$2,125) per month. The villages now had electricity and farm-to-market roads, and many farmers had been able to improve their houses, or buy cassette players and television sets. By 1996, the PBSP Program Evaluation Report cited that poverty incidence in the area had been reduced by 21 percent.

PROGRAM EXPANSION   PBSP's progress in the three villages encouraged the expansion of its program to two additional villages that were adjacent to the original three. These were Babag and Pong-ol Sibugay villages. The Australian Agency for International Development (AusAid) funded the community development and reforestation costs from 1993 to 1996.

PHASE III (1994–1996): BUSINESS TAKES A STAND FOR COMMUNITY'S LAND TENURE AND WATERSHED PROTECTION

As the farmers tilled their lands to produce high-yielding crops and nurtured trees that also promised future income, they began to express with greater urgency their desire to have a claim to the land. The farmers had always dreamed of legal tenure over the land where their houses and farms stood. Accordingly, in 1994, PBSP adjusted its program goals to include land security. Later that year, 17 farmers acquired Certificates of Stewardship contracts from the Department of Environment and Natural Resources, and the other farmers started submitting applications as well.[7]

Conflict arose, however, in May 1994, when the farmers of the Sudlon II Farmers Livelihood and Training Service Foundation (SUFALTRAS), one of the three cooperatives with which PBSP was working, saw a bulldozer enter the Sudlon National Park in the Mananga reserve. It destroyed their trees and crops. "We could not do anything then," said Dindo Pagatpat, the president of SUFALTRAS. "We had no warning."[8] The bulldozers belonged to a large, Cebu-based trading company that was not a member of PBSP. The company claimed that it was the legal owner of the land, and it was clearing the land to make way for a golf course. Meanwhile, the company had asked their employee cooperative, the Gabi Multi-Purpose Cooperative, to be caretaker of the area.[9] The Gabi Multi-Purpose Cooperative sued the SUFALTRAS farmers, alleging that it owned the land that the SUFALTRAS farmers occupied.

A court battle ensued, the results of which are still pending five years later. The local PBSP Board gave the farmers full support for their cause. As one member of the Board noted, PBSP had poured a lot of resources

7. The stewardship contract is for a period of 25 years, granted by the Department of Environment and Natural Resources to select families long residing in the area and adopting sustainable farming practices.

8. Interview with farmer leader Dindo Pagatpat, August 1998, Center for Rural Technology Development, Laguna.

9. SUFALTRAS farmers claimed that the Gabi cooperative members had never lived in their area.

into the hillyland project and had accomplished a great deal already, which would be wasted if the land issue was not resolved in the farmers' favor.

The incident between SUFALTRAS farmers and the trading company was but one of several similar conflicts erupting in the hillyland, as tensions were mounting between groups moving to develop land in the watershed areas and those who advocated preservation of the critical resource. "Cebu's sectors realized that they all had a stake in the watersheds," commented Aurora Tolentino, then PBSP's executive director. "They had to be able to sit down together and ensure that there would be water now and in the future for everyone, and not just a few."[10]

As a result, 34 NGOs and civil society organizations joined together in 1995 to form a water lobby. Cebu Uniting for Sustainable Water (CUSW) was created to "formulate and institutionalize an integrated resource and land use master plan for the Metro Cebu area, with special considerations for water resources management."[11] CUSW drew up a Watershed Development Management Framework to influence policy making regarding the upland resources and to prevent development of the Mananga area without due consideration of the impact on the environment and on the farmers living there. The PBSP regional Board took an active role in this new organization as the business sector's representative to CUSW.

CONCLUSION

The Cebu Hillyland Development Program was a successful model of partnership for environmental protection and community development. It drew on the resources of the Cebu City government; the three farmers' organizations, representing some 330 upland households; and the business community, comprised of more than 60 private companies and at least 700 volunteers. PBSP played a critical role, acting as an intermediary between these different sectors. It mobilized business resources through its fund-raising campaigns, tapped schools and hospitals for in-kind contributions, and organized business executives and employees to volunteer their time and talent. PBSP also mobilized upland community

10. Interview with Ma. Aurora F. Tolentino, July 1998, PBSP, Manila.

11. Lulu Coles, "Initiatives toward Management in Cebu," Paper prepared for the Upland NGO Assistance Committee's National Consultative Meeting, August 1998, Antipolo.

resources, enabling the farmers' cooperatives to become more productive and to participate in reforestation. Four years into the program, PBSP also assumed the role of legal advisor to one of the farmers' organizations in a land dispute, thus taking on the role of advocate for the farmers' land tenure and for watershed protection.

In coordinating the efforts of government, business, and community organizations, PBSP was able to demonstrate its organizational strength and influence. That strength derived from a number of factors that proved critical to the success of the project. First, the PBSP Board, both at the national and local levels, showed leadership and commitment to the principle of corporate social responsibility. Second, PBSP was able to have an impact by pooling the resources of its corporate members, drawing on their financial, material, and technical resources, as well as their influence. These resources were also leveraged by PBSP to attract resources from additional donors. Third, the professional development staff was able to draw on a combination of social development skills and business discipline for effective management of programs. Fourth, the network of local NGO and community partners, mostly trained by PBSP, widened the reach of the projects and assured sustainability through community ownership of the projects. Finally, PBSP's established connections with a wide range of stakeholders, from prominent politicians and business leaders to grass-roots leaders, enabled it to identify and resolve various issues. As Roberto Calingo, PBSP's current executive director notes, "There is a need for greater consensus among key actors in resource management. Partnership building takes off from this key success factor. This must survive the test of time and interest."[12]

Using these strengths, PBSP provided business with practical opportunities for involvement in social and environmental problems. After PBSP showed what was possible to do in the three villages, two member companies, San Miguel Corporation and Aboitiz Co., decided to adopt other villages on their own. PBSP also introduced business to the experience of working with other sectors toward an identified common goal. Through the Cebu Hillyland experience, businesses were challenged to consider their own corporate citizenship and to look beyond their own interests to the interests of society and the environment.

---

12. Interview with Roberto Calingo, May 19, 1999, PBSP, Manila.

6 British Petroleum Partnership with Save the Children and Fauna and Flora International

Nguyen Van Thanh
and
Tadashi Yamamoto

BRITISH PETROLEUM (BP) is one of the largest oil and petrochemicals companies in the world.[1] It is actively involved in all phases of the oil and gas industry in some 70 countries, is the largest producer of oil in the United States, and is the biggest oil and gas operator in the U.K. sector of the North Sea. In the past, BP has had an alliance with Statoil, which is Norway's state oil and gas enterprise and the country's largest company. Statoil is the leading producer of oil and gas in the North Sea, and also has an extensive and expanding network of international exploration ventures.

Vietnam is one of a number of areas around the world where BP and Statoil have worked together in exploring for oil and gas, and although the formal BP/Statoil Alliance no longer exists, the two companies still work together in that country. They have been investing in Vietnam since the beginning of 1989, and are now considered among the earliest and most active foreign investors to have come to Vietnam. Both companies have emphasized community involvement activities in their worldwide operations, and, at the initiative of BP's Barry Bidston, manager in charge of

The authors gratefully acknowledge the assistance of Ngyen Quoc Binh and Susan Hubbard.

1. In December 1998, BP merged with the American corporation Amoco, to form the world's third largest oil company, BP Amoco. Four months later, BP Amoco merged with the Atlantic Richfield Company (ARCO) of Los Angeles, forming BP Amoco–ARCO. For the purpose of this chapter, however, we will refer only to the premerger activities and philosophies of British Petroleum.

95

community relations in Vietnam, they have collaborated to contribute to Vietnamese society.

This chapter deals with two cases in which the BP/Statoil Alliance worked in partnership with nongovernmental organizations (NGOs) to address social welfare and environmental problems in Vietnam: the Poverty Alleviation and Nutrition Program in Thanh Hoa Province, run by Save the Children of the United States, and the Cuc Phuong National Park Conservation Project, conducted with Fauna and Flora International (FFI) of Cambridge, England. In both cases, Vietnamese organizations such as local women's unions, farmers' unions, and youth unions have played a significant role. Also involved in the projects was the People's Aid Coordination Committee (PACCOM) under the Vietnam Union of Friendship Organizations, which is assigned by the government to facilitate philanthropic and community activities of foreign nongovernmental organizations and corporations in Vietnam.

PHILANTHROPIC ACTIVITIES
OF BRITISH PETROLEUM

BP spends an estimated US$64.9 million annually on philanthropic and community activities worldwide.[2] It has only been in recent years, however, that the company has attempted to approach these activities in a more systematic manner and to elucidate a more comprehensive corporate philosophy.

In March 1998, BP published a booklet titled "What We Stand For. . . ." According to John Gore, director of external affairs and communications, this booklet represents the first comprehensive document produced by BP to outline a set of corporate values that should be manifested in corporate behavior.[3] Going well beyond a "code of conduct," the booklet is designed to convey the corporation's beliefs and philosophy "to diverse sectors such as government, politicians, media, NGOs, and so forth, in

2. Of this amount, approximately 24 percent is used for community development, 23 percent for education, 21 percent for arts and culture, 9 percent for the environment, and 23 percent for other purposes.

3. John Gore and Jeremy Nicholls, manager of community affairs, Global Business Center, were interviewed by Tadashi Yamamoto at BP headquarters in London on March 18, 1998. Barry Bidston, manager, BP Exploration Operating Company, was interviewed by Hideko Katsumata and Mio Kawashima of the Japan Center for International Exchange on January 14, 1998, in Ho Chi Minh City.

a consistent and integrated manner." As an upstream business in the energy field heavily invested in exploration and development of natural resources, BP considers its relationships with the government and the environmental community to be extremely important. The traditional approach at BP, according to Gore, was to have different departments or individuals dealing with different audiences, but it had become increasingly difficult to compartmentalize the company's approach to diverse sectors.

"What We Stand For . . ." spells out BP's business policies, focusing on five areas: ethical conduct; employees; relationships; health, safety, and environmental performance; and finance and control. Emphasizing that "Our policy commitments are the foundation on which we will build and conduct our business," the booklet outlines the ways in which those commitments are to be carried out: (1) by understanding the needs and aspirations of individuals, customers, contractors, suppliers, partners, governments, and nongovernmental organizations, (2) by conducting activities in ways which benefit all those with whom BP has relationships, (3) by fulfilling obligations as a responsible member of the societies in which BP operates, and (4) by demonstrating respect for human dignity and the rights of individuals. Compiled with the participation of some 350 top managers, the booklet, along with background materials and a video presentation, has since been disseminated throughout the organization and its overseas offices. In addition, a group of three to four experts has been sent around to the corporate offices to discuss the booklet with employees.

Prior to "What We Stand For . . . ," BP had published "BP in the Community 1996," which was the company's first attempt to depict the overall size and scope of its community affairs program. That publication was designed to reinforce the potential benefit of community relationships to people inside and outside the BP organization, and to demonstrate BP's "belief in the importance of building a shared agenda with community partners, based on the idea of mutual advantage, which we see as the best basis for sound, long-term relationships."

In what might at first appear to be a paradoxical choice, at the same time that it was undertaking these recent efforts to form a more cohesive, overall philosophy for its corporate philanthropy and community affairs activities, BP also started an initiative around 1995 to decentralize these activities, shifting responsibility for deciding the areas and scope of community affairs programs from the headquarters in London to some

90 regional and local units in 70 countries. Although there are some general guidelines, the priorities and budget size are determined by the local managers. While BP's 1996 annual report focuses on the areas of environment, education, and community development in the two full pages allocated to its community affairs activities, according to Gore this was simply a convenient way of trying to categorize BP's overall community affairs efforts. Some units actually emphasize cultural activities, while others devote resources primarily to poverty alleviation.

In the company's atomized managerial environment, needs and opportunities are diverse, and it is difficult to specify a single set of guidelines for community affairs. It is even difficult to set guidelines on a regional basis, because each region is made up of many countries with diverse cultural backgrounds and at different stages of development. BP feels that giving the local units a freer hand allows them to better identify appropriate activities for a given community and enables local managers to express their commitment to serving the community or the host country more effectively. As noted by Jeremy Nicholls, manager of community affairs in the Global Business Center in the London headquarters, the company "cannot dictate a single way to do things under different circumstances."

The method of carrying out community affairs is also determined by the local managers. Local units are able to employ professionals with background in philanthropy or NGOs, and there are about such 30 specialists worldwide, including Barry Bidston in Vietnam. In general, Nicholls recognizes the value of having experienced professionals on the community affairs staff, but he also believes that local managers are sometimes best equipped to consider the overall relationship with the government, local community, people's organizations, and others.

BP IN VIETNAM

BP, along with Statoil, has been investing in Vietnam since 1989 and is now considered to be among the earliest and most active foreign investors to have come to Vietnam. Their combined investment has totaled over US$500 million thus far. The BP/Statoil Alliance started conducting community activities in Vietnam in 1990, motivated by a belief in the importance of demonstrating good corporate citizenship, and by the desire to enhance their corporate image and reputation by working in partnership with the community. To date, roughly US$3 million has been spent on community support programs in Vietnam.

Corporate philanthropic activities are conducted by a Public Affairs Team with the involvement of some 20 officers and staff members from diverse departments of the companies. The team and its programs are co-ordinated by Barry Bidston, who arrived in Vietnam in 1993. He serves as the BP/Statoil external affairs manager, based in Ho Chi Minh City, and reports to the BP country office in Hanoi to coordinate the projects.

According to Bidston, one of the basic principles of the community affairs program is the need to establish partnerships with government authorities. This is particularly true in Vietnam, where it is necessary for foreign corporations and foreign NGOs to receive government approval. Quite often, the government designates what kind of programs the organizations should be conducting, and it is important to conform with such guidelines and establish trust with the government authorities.

In entering into community projects, BP applies three criteria, namely that the proposed program: (1) should have a measurable impact, (2) should become a "national model" for others to emulate, and (3) should be sustainable in due course with local community resources. BP generally prefers to be the sole sponsor of programs in order to get the maximum benefit from the activities, and tries to involve employees where possible. BP in Vietnam has also established internal guidelines for its community affairs activities to focus on education, community, environment, and self-help projects.

There are currently four major BP/Statoil projects in Vietnam, each receiving a financial contribution of more than US$100,000 annually.[4] Two of these cases—a poverty alleviation program with Save the Children and a nature conservation project with Fauna and Flora International—will be described in detail below. The third major project is a Disaster Management Unit in the Mekong Delta, where BP/Statoil initially sponsored a computer-based communication system linking 11 flood-prone Mekong Delta provinces to Ho Chi Minh City and Hanoi. The objective is to materially assist disaster mitigation and management associated with annual flooding, which has become more severe due to deforestation of the Mekong catchment area in neighboring countries. The project is carried out with the United Nations Development Program and the

---

4. BP provides two-thirds of the Alliance project funding and Statoil one-third.

Ministry of Agriculture and Rural Development. The fourth major project that BP/Statoil supports is the Marcel Loos Memorial Business Course at Da Nang University. The course, taught in English, covers modern accounting and business skills that are required for the transition to a market economy. This project is run in association with Quang Nam Da Nang People's Committee.

CASE 1: POVERTY ALLEVIATION AND NUTRITION PROGRAM IN THANH HOA

BACKGROUND

Vietnam has a four-tiered administrative structure with central, provincial, district, and communal levels. There are nearly 10,000 communes (the most basic administrative unit) throughout Vietnam, with an average population of 6,000 per commune.[5] Each commune is organized around a Commune Communist Party that plays a leadership role in all commune activities, a Commune People's Committee that serves as an executive and management agency, and "mass organizations," such as schoolchildren leagues, youth leagues, women's unions, and senior citizens' unions, that mobilize people to participate in community activities.

Since the early 1960s, Vietnam has had a communal health service system with a health center in each commune and a network of village health workers. This system was sustained by the existence of Commune Agriculture Collective Farms as a funding source. In 1986, however, Vietnam adopted an economic reform policy that shifted the country from a centrally planned socialist economic system toward a market economy. In rural areas, this meant that the Commune Agriculture Collective Farms ceased playing a role in community economic management and wealth distribution. As a result, each commune had to find its own way to maintain community health services. In addition, since 1989, private medical service, commercial sales of pharmaceuticals, and fees for medical care service were sanctioned by the government. These changes severely strained the traditional system, and by 1993 even the Central Committee of the Communist Party was ready to declare the collapse of the communal health system. The following year, however, witnessed the introduction

5. Tran Tuan, "Historical Development of Primary Health Care in Vietnam: Lessons for the Future," Research Paper No. 102 (Boston: Takemi Program in International Health, Harvard School of Public Health), 1995.

of a national salary system for local leaders and commune health center staff, and a renewed government commitment to strengthening the public health system, which gradually began to show signs of recovery.

Nonetheless, despite the recent improvements in the health system, malnutrition remains a serious problem in Vietnam. According to 1995 figures from the National Institute of Nutrition, 45 percent of children under the age of five were malnourished, and the rate of babies born with low birthweight was between 12 percent and 20 percent. The government has therefore adopted a National Plan of Action for Nutrition, which aims to reduce the prevalence of malnutrition in children under the age of five to less than 30 percent by the year 2000. It was in this context that an American NGO, Save the Children, chose to focus its efforts in Vietnam on the problem of malnutrition.

SAVE THE CHILDREN

Save the Children was founded in 1932 and is registered in the United States as a nonprofit, nonpolitical, and nonsectarian organization operating interrelated programs in education, health, economic opportunities, and emergency response in 35 countries. Save the Children's mission is to create lasting, positive change in the lives of disadvantaged children.

Save the Children was one of the first foreign NGOs operating in Vietnam to be granted a permit by the Committee for Non-Governmental Organization Affairs of Vietnam for the establishment of a representative office, the highest status for a foreign NGO recognized by the Government of Vietnam. The Vietnam office of Save the Children is based in Hanoi and is run by two expatriate staff and 16 Vietnamese staff. The mission of Save the Children in Vietnam is "to measurably and sustainably enhance the quality of life of women, children and their families." To do so, the organization sought to create a commune-level development program that "could make an immediate, measurable and sustainable impact on malnutrition, before waiting for other causal factors, such as water supply, sanitation, structural poverty, etc., to be addressed."[6] This program would then serve as a model that other communes could replicate.

Save the Children first came to Vietnam in 1990. It contacted the Ministry of Foreign Affairs and was introduced to PACCOM under the Vietnam Union of Friendship Organizations, which is assigned by the government

6. "Save the Children Viet Nam Office Program Plan, FY1998–2000."

to facilitate foreign NGOs' activities in Vietnam. Save the Children expressed its desire to help the country's neediest citizens, and was briefed by PACCOM about the general situation in Vietnam at that time, and especially about the situation in the rural areas of the country. Save the Children was then introduced by PACCOM to two provinces located in central Vietnam that were classified at the time as the poorest provinces. These areas had very low per capita income, poor infrastructure, and were most prone to natural disasters. Following a site visit to assess the needs in these provinces, Save the Children chose the province of Thanh Hoa to begin its project.

POVERTY ALLEVIATION AND NUTRITION PROGRAM

In 1990, Save the Children initiated a partnership with BP when its former director met with BP officials in London to discuss plans to create a rural development model in Vietnam. At that time, BP made an initial funding commitment of three years to set up the project.

The Poverty Alleviation and Nutrition Program (PANP) began in 1991 with a pilot project in four communes of Quang Xuong District, located in Thanh Hoa Province, roughly 400 kilometers south of Hanoi. Save the Children first conducted a needs assessment, which was carried out in close collaboration with the local women's unions, farmers' unions, and the people's committees. This revealed very important information on the conditions existing in the communes. First, they found that one out of every three children under the age of three years was suffering from second or third degree malnutrition (i.e., moderate to severe malnutrition) and was in danger of physical and intellectual stunting. This was perhaps not surprising for a population so impoverished that most only have sufficient rice (their main staple) for seven months a year and must subsist on sweet potatoes and cassava for the remaining five months. The farmers, too poor to buy fertilizer, were obtaining extremely low yields despite their intensive labor.

The second important finding was related to the state of the health care system in these communes. The health care centers were dilapidated, with neither running water nor latrines. The annual budget for medicine in each health center, serving populations of between 4,000 and 6,000 each, was only US$0.40–US$0.70 per head, and the health workers, who had not received salaries in several months, spent more time working in the fields than in the centers.

Initial discussions with community leaders revealed a litany of inter-related and mutually exacerbating problems: The communes were extremely poor owing to low agricultural productivity and were therefore unable to support health services. Low agricultural productivity also meant that family consumption of rice was extremely low, and, consequently, many children were hungry and suffering from malnutrition. Despite the numerous problems that existed, the consensus of all concerned was that the first priority should be to address the mounting hunger experienced by the poorest of the poor, and particularly the children.

This initial challenge provided a classical development dilemma: The need was immediate, but response based solely on food distribution would create dependency and a "relief mentality." It would not produce a sustainable solution to the underlying problem. As a first program intervention, it was critical that Save the Children demonstrate responsiveness to the needs of the community, but within a "development" rather then a "relief" context. The finding of widespread second- and third-degree malnutrition in the communes posed two immediate challenges: the rehabilitation of affected children and, of equal importance, the identification of a strategy to enable their families to independently maintain the enhanced nutritional status after rehabilitation.

The idea behind the PANP originated with a discovery made in a nutritional baseline survey. That survey established that there were indeed some children from extremely poor families who were not malnourished —what was termed "positive deviants." Further study comparing the different feeding patterns of poor parents with malnourished children and those of parents with adequately nourished children revealed that the latter group was adding sweet potato greens and small shrimps and crabs caught in the rice paddies to their children's diet. These appeared to provide the key to their superior nutritional status. Although abundantly available, these foods are not traditionally fed to young children.

This discovery served as the core of the nutritional component of the program. The action to be taken was simple and cost effective. The children who were identified as malnourished were invited to attend a two-week Nutrition Education Rehabilitation Program session, in which their mothers or caregivers were taught by health volunteers to prepare a calorie-sufficient meal using shrimps, crabs, and greens. Daily messages stressing the importance of these additions reinforced the newly acquired feeding patterns and were soon internalized by the participants. The results of the program during 1991 proved to be quite successful. The unique study of Save the Children has enabled the community to use its own resources to address the problem of malnutrition.

Based on these results, the Nutrition Education Rehabilitation Program has continued to be carried out successfully in combination with other components of a comprehensive PANP program. Strategically, the program first enables the community to implement projects that specifically address the problem of malnutrition. The focus then broadens to enable the community to embark on the prevention of malnutrition and to understand the importance of women's health as a personal and community asset.

Since the initial three-year commitment, BP has been pleased with the outcome of the project, and has continued to fund Save the Children. Throughout the implementation of PANP, however, BP's participation in the project has gone well beyond its financial contribution. Save the Children submits its periodic program reports to BP, and BP occasionally sends observers to evaluate the program's impact on the communities and to offer advice and recommendations. BP has also developed with Save the Children in Hanoi a common program for their staff development.

PARTNERSHIP WITH LOCAL CITIZENS

With the strong belief that, given a little help, communities can find solutions to their own problems, the primary objective of the Save the Children program has been to create a sustainable, measurable reduction in malnutrition, using a model that can be replicated throughout the country. Therefore, maximum community involvement has been encouraged from the very beginning. Save the Children has worked very closely with the women's unions, the farmers' associations, and the people's committees at the communal level in the process. Health volunteers were selected within the communes, and provincial, district, and commune level medical personnel have played a central role in medical intervention efforts.

The training of local citizens is believed to be one of the critical factors in the success of the program. The Living University was established by Save the Children in 1994 to enable health volunteers, government officials, women's union staff, and other groups to replicate the program on their own. The Living University also provides participants with an opportunity to learn about health care and nutrition counseling skills. The courses are conducted in areas where PANP is in progress, thus giving the participants a chance to observe the program and practice their skills.

By May 1998, more than 2,600 health volunteers and 750 government staff from 15 provinces had attended the Living University and are now implementing PANP by themselves in more than 200 communes across the country.

It is important to emphasize again the fact that the villagers, who are all volunteers, have been directly involved in implementing the nutrition program. During the first year of the partnership, which constituted the pilot period, funding went directly to the communities. Save the Children took on the role of implementing agency, but it collaborated closely with the villagers. During the second phase, Save the Children staff trained people to work with the villagers. During the third phase, Save the Children staff are working with district and provincial organizations, such as the Committee for Protection and Care for Children, health organizations, and unions. This community involvement is critical for creating a long-term, self-sustaining program to combat malnutrition.

CASE 2: CUC PHUONG NATIONAL PARK CONSERVATION PROJECT

BACKGROUND

Cuc Phuong National Park was established in 1962, and contains approximately 180 square kilometers of relatively undisturbed subtropical and tropical evergreen forest. It remains one of the largest forests in northwest Vietnam. At its inception, Cuc Phuong supported some 64 mammal species, 319 bird species, and 33 reptile species. It was also estimated to have insects from at least 1,800 species. More recently, Cuc Phuong was identified as a "hot spot" for bat diversity after surveys recorded a total of 37 species—more than have been found at any other single site in Southeast Asia. One of the most notable features of Cuc Phuong is that it is the only known protected area where one can find the Delacouri langur, one of Asia's most endangered primates. The park is also home to several other threatened species, including the little known Owston's palm civet and the red-collared woodpecker.

In addition to its biological value, Cuc Phuong's natural resources are extremely important to numerous communities situated in and around the park. As a virtual ecological island amidst the intensely farmed surrounding lowlands, Cuc Phuong provides important watershed services to these subsistence farmers, as well as many timber and nontimber products. Hunting pressures in the park are intense and, as a result, some large species of mammals and two bird species have been eradicated from the area in recent years. Poaching threatens the park's tiny Delacouri langur population with imminent extinction, while a host of other activities such as firewood collection, grazing of buffalo, agricultural encroachment, and harvesting of nontimber forest products continue to threaten the integrity of the park and its wildlife. The key problems are that local community use of the park's resources is not sustainable and that these communities' needs are not being considered in the park's management and protection strategies. These problems became the focus of a project conducted through a partnership between BP and a British NGO, Fauna and Flora International (FFI).

FAUNA AND FLORA INTERNATIONAL

Founded in 1903, FFI is the world's oldest international conservation organization. With headquarters in Cambridge, England, FFI's mission is to safeguard the future of endangered species of animals and plants worldwide. It currently manages a number of major programs and supports many more by focusing on key conservation issues in nearly 100 countries. FFI's activities worldwide include biodiversity surveys and assessments; development of protected area management; species conservation programs; global strategic planning for threatened species; conservation campaigns; institution-strengthening activities to develop in-country capacity; and publication of quarterly journals, magazines, and newsletters.

FFI first came to Vietnam in 1995 and, with the agreement of the Ministry of Agriculture and Rural Development, launched four projects in 1996. The first project, which will be discussed in detail in this case study, was the Cuc Phuong National Park Conservation Project, funded by the BP/Statoil Alliance in Vietnam. The remaining projects included a survey on Vietnam's vanishing elephants, a project to conserve endangered species on the border areas between Vietnam, Laos, and Cambodia, and another conservation project that aimed to build capacity within Vietnam for breeding critically endangered species.

CUC PHUONG NATIONAL PARK CONSERVATION PROJECT

The Cuc Phuong project was initiated by the former project manger of FFI, Shane Rosenthal, who identified a need for further research into the economic and social situation in the buffer zone surrounding the park as a result of evidence that forest resources from Cuc Phuong were being exploited locally at unsustainable rates. Rosenthal and FFI approached BP and other potential funders. They contacted John Addy, who was in charge of environmental coordination in BP's London headquarters. Addy had received a number of other proposals for environmental projects in Vietnam but had yet to find a project adequate for BP support. FFI's proposal interested Addy, and he decided to consult with Nguyen Thi Lien Ha, project development coordinator for the BP office in Vietnam. Ha is responsible for ensuring that the environmental performance of BP in Vietnam is in compliance with the guidelines of BP headquarters and of the Vietnamese authorities.

The final decision to work with FFI was made in Vietnam, and funding came from the Vietnam office. Although BP had had a long history of cooperation with FFI headquarters, BP Vietnam had not had any previous connection with FFI in Vietnam, which, like FFI offices in other countries, is fairly independent. The idea of the Cuc Phuong conservation project attracted BP Vietnam's interest, however, since it fit well with BP's motto of trying to be a responsible corporate citizen by working in partnership with the community where it operates.

A project proposal was sent to the Forest Protection Department under the Ministry of Agriculture and Rural Development for approval. Recognizing the need to develop cooperation with international organizations to help protect the park, the Department accepted the proposal, and the project got under way.

The Cuc Phuong National Park Conservation Project is a multifaceted conservation initiative implemented and administered by FFI in cooperation with Cuc Phuong National Park. The park was chosen to be a long-term project of FFI in Vietnam as it is the country's first and best-known national park, with a very favorable location only 60 kilometers southwest of Hanoi. Given its long history, Cuc Phuong is in many ways regarded as a model for protected areas in Vietnam and thus plays a key role in influencing the development of other conservation areas. Its fame and location were also factors in BP's choice to fund the project.

In this partnership, FFI received an annual budget of US$120,000 from BP/Statoil for the first two years (1996–1998), making up about 60 percent of the total budget for the project. In addition to financial assistance, BP/Statoil takes part in the project's Steering Committee, comprised of one representative each from FFI headquarters and FFI Vietnam, three from the park itself, and two from the BP/Statoil Alliance. The Committee meets every six months for discussion and decisions on the action plan of the project. BP/Statoil also sends its staff regularly to the project site to visit and learn about community development activities, which is part of staff training strategy. In addition, BP/Statoil occasionally helps FFI by providing satellite information on the conservation issues related to the project's activities, and with the publication of brochures for the park. FFI, through the Steering Committee, submits regular executive reports to BP/Statoil and submits financial reports directly to BP's headquarters in the United Kingdom.

The project consists of five components. They are complementary in their objectives and together form an integrated approach to the improvement of conservation at Cuc Phuong through increased knowledge and local participation in resource management.

SOCIOECONOMIC STUDY OF COMMUNITY RESOURCE USE   The objective of this component is to provide detailed information and analysis concerning such questions as who collects resources, to what extent these are marketed and contribute to a given household's welfare, and other socioeconomic aspects of Cuc Phuong. Such information enables the project to respond effectively to excessive resource use and encourage the involvement of local communities in day-to-day management activities, by offering local residents incentives for conservation.

CONSERVATION AWARENESS PROGRAM   The main objective of this program is to increase awareness of the park's conservation priorities and help modify local use of its resources by involving local communities in activities and discussions focusing on the role of the park and its value as a conservation area. This component focuses on a number of target groups, including consumers and protectors—or in broad terms, local residents and forest guards—among whom schoolchildren and their teachers are a critical audience. Training classes for children and teachers are conducted by FFI's staff in collaboration with the park's personnel and the schools in the area around the park. Conservation clubs are also established in a number of communities to encourage the participation of the residents.

VISITOR EDUCATION PROGRAM   As the park receives about 20,000 visitors yearly, this component aims to develop a conservation awareness and nature interpretation program to improve the educational value of visits to the park, and to increase public awareness of environmental conservation and the importance of Vietnam's protected areas. The program focuses mainly on students from Hanoi's primary, secondary, and tertiary schools, who form the largest portion of the park's visitors.

BIOLOGICAL RESEARCH AND INVENTORY PROGRAM In response to the need for basic studies to evaluate and classify the park's ecology and biodiversity, research on the park's flora and fauna is conducted by Vietnamese and foreign specialists. This research is valuable in scientific terms and as an input for the park's natural resource management planning.

STUDY, CONSERVATION, AND ECOLOGY OF CIVETS Cuc Phuong is home to five civet species that are believed to play a very important role in the forest ecosystem, for example in seed dispersal and forest regeneration, about which virtually nothing is known. The purpose of this component is to investigate the ecology and conservation of the Owston's palm civet, and to examine its life in conjunction with other civet species.

PARTNERSHIP WITH LOCAL CITIZENS

Currently, FFI has a full-time staff of eight, including two expatriates and six Vietnamese. In addition, eight personnel from the park are working as program officers on a part-time basis. As the nature of the work requires field participation, all Vietnamese staff, including the park personnel, have received standardized in-the-field training conducted by FFI's experts from within Vietnam and abroad. FFI's strategy is to localize its personnel, and it has provided one Vietnamese program officer with a special on-the-job training course to enable him to replace the project manager, an expatriate, in early 1999.

In carrying out the conservation program, FFI emphasizes partnership with local citizens. It works closely with the youth unions within two districts where the program is active, as well as with many village and commune leaders and with teachers within the 15 communes surrounding the park. A wide range of training courses have been organized in the communes within the framework of education programs for teachers, youth union members, and the park staff, as well as a biology program for the park's scientific staff, representatives from national institutions, and forestry college graduates.

FFI's work with local citizens has been commended by BP, which emphasizes such community-level partnerships. According to Doug Hendries, FFI administrator of the program at the park, working on conservation efforts with the surrounding people is the biggest challenge.[7] The area around the park is densely populated, and the people living around the park are poor and dependent on resources from within the park for their daily survival. For that reason, BP has placed high priority on improving education and economic development in the buffer zone around the park.

CONCLUSION

The two cases described represent partnerships between foreign corporations and international NGOs. In addition, however, there has been significant participation by state institutions at the national and local levels. There also has been active participation by local villagers through such people's organizations as youth unions and women's unions, which may not be exactly the same as NGOs in the Western sense but nonetheless share many similar characteristics. Thus, these two cases provide a unique model of multisectoral partnership wherein each actor has played a significant role and has satisfied its needs and missions.

One factor that facilitated such a partnership was the willingness of the Vietnamese authorities to accept the participation of foreign corporations and NGOs. In his address to the Association of Sponsors of the Poor Patients of Ho Chin Minh City, Prime Minister Phan Van Khai stated, "You have been very active and devoted to helping poor patients. But, as reported at the National Assembly recently, about 16 percent of the population remains poor. Therefore, you will need more means to cure a larger number of children and adults, and I suggest you appeal for more funds at home and abroad."[8] The Vietnam Union of Friendship Organization, with the People's Aid Coordination Committee as its functional body, has been appointed to be the standing agency for nongovernmental affairs. Cooperating with foreign entities working on social issues and promoting partnerships between the state sector—both central government and local administration—the private sector of business and financial institutions, and the voluntary sector of NGOs and community-based organizations have been some of the main activities of the People's Aid Coordination Committee.

A relatively new phenomenon of greater participation by people's

7. Interview with Doug Hendries at Cuc Phuong National Park by Ngyen Quoc Binh, Susan Hubbard, and Mio Kawashima, August 4, 1998.

8. *Vietnam News*, November 23, 1998.

organizations in social issues has surfaced as well. This is understood to be associated with the abolition of the subsidy system and the decline in state expenditures on some elements of social services. As a result, while the state continues to play the key role in addressing social issues, the involvement of citizens has become increasingly important. The Communist Party recognized the need "to vigorously turn toward the grass roots to develop their organization, consolidate and socialize their activities, train and forge their personnel," and proposed that "the State should promulgate a law on the founding of associations and facilitate the operation of people's organizations."[9] In this new environment, international NGOs have become very active in Vietnam. By the end of 1998, there were 482 foreign NGOs conducting projects and programs in Vietnam, of which 324 were registered with the Committee for NGO Affairs, the new administrative body. Of these, 40 NGOs have been officially permitted to open representative offices and 51 have been given the status of project office.

The apparent success of the two cases taken up here can be attributed to the strategy of both Save the Children and Fauna and Flora International, as well as to that of the BP/Statoil Alliance, to work closely with the government authorities and local organizations. Both of these international NGOs have a philosophy of working with local citizens, and their offices are mostly staffed by Vietnamese nationals with only a limited number of expatriates. This pattern is also common to most of BP's community programs around the world. As noted in its publication titled "BP in the Community 1996," BP believes that allowing local operations to develop programs in response to local needs and circumstances "is the best way to ensure that what we do is relevant and meaningful for the business and the community concerned." The fact that a shared operational philosophy existed among the corporate and NGO partners seems to have been an essential factor in the success of the partnerships.

Finally, it is important to point out that professionals both in the corporations and the NGOs have played a critical role in forging the effective partnerships. It goes without saying that initiating and managing joint activities in different cultural and sociopolitical settings is not a simple task. In the final analysis, these two cases demonstrate the skill and dedication of the people on the ground to working effectively with Vietnamese authorities and people in the communities.

9. Communist Party of Vietnam, Eighth National Party Congress, The GIOI, Hanoi, 1996.

7 Bankers Trust Barangay Improvement Project

Hiroshi Peter Kamura

IN 1996, when representatives from the Bankers Trust Foundation and its nonprofit partner, Philippine Business for Social Progress (PBSP), first visited the Barangay Tipas section of Taguig in Metro Manila, they found a neighborhood that epitomized the city's urban blight. Poverty was rampant. Although many of the men worked in nearby factories, the pay was low and the women had no livelihood skills that would help them augment the family income. A daycare center had been set up to teach indigent children, but the structure was primitive and the children often spilled out into the streets. The entire area was surrounded by murky, stagnant water that was a breeding gound for mosquitoes and water-borne diseases. The only route in and out of Barangay Tipas was a makeshift bridge of wooden planks.

Two years later, through the efforts of a corporate-NGO partnership between the Bankers Trust Foundation, PBSP, and a second Philippine NGO, that run-down section of town had become a model for urban development efforts. The project succeeded in organizing the community, constructing sanitation facilities and other infrastructure, conducting job training and livelihood development activities, and improving schools and daycare. So impressed was the community with Bankers Trust's commitment to this project that it named a newly paved thoroughfare after the company. Bankers Trust's experience with this and other corporate-NGO partnerships provides valuable insight into what enables such collaborative endeavors to succeed.

BANKERS TRUST COMPANY:
THE PHILOSOPHY OF COMMUNITY INVOLVEMENT

BACKGROUND

Bankers Trust Company, founded in 1903, is a leading global financial services corporation with headquarters in New York City and more than 80 offices in 55 countries around the world.[1] The eighth largest bank in the United States, it employs approximately 20,000 personnel worldwide and makes more than half its earnings abroad. Bankers Trust is one of world's largest investment managers, with revenues reaching US$6.25 billion in 1997.

Throughout Bankers Trust's history, the company has been engaged in philanthropic giving, providing funds in a fairly unfocused manner to arts organizations, museums, hospitals, and children's charities. In the 1980s, when the company's orientation fundamentally changed from that of a traditional commercial bank to a more diversified financial services firm, Bankers Trust began to rethink its corporate social responsibility programs. As a result, "community development" became the strategic core of a set of new philanthropic initiatives. The company also decided to establish a foundation to implement this new agenda, and thus created the Bankers Trust Foundation in 1986.

The programs of the Foundation have centered around capacity building in needy communities—"supporting the entrepreneurial, grass-roots efforts of local citizens, improving educational opportunities, and providing resources that go beyond charity to find solutions to complex social problems."[2] Bankers Trust's work in this area has earned it a reputation in the United States as a pioneer in defining new methods of addressing the needs of impoverished inner-city communities. Innovative financing programs are helping rebuild these communities with new housing for the homeless and home ownership opportunities for low-income working families. Bankers Trust is also investing in the creation of locally owned businesses in partnership with the Ford Foundation, and helping to build

1. In 1998, it was announced that Deutsche Bank would acquire Bankers Trust, effective as of June 1999. The impact of this merger on the company's philanthropic programs remains to be seen.

2. Interview with Page Chapman III, president of the Bankers Trust Foundation, at the Bankers Trust Foundation, New York, July 20, 1998. Also from the Bankers Trust brochure, "A Strategy for Global Corporate Citizenship."

capable and enduring nonprofit organizations, such as the Central Harlem Local Development Corporation and the South Bronx Overall Economic Development Corporation.

CORPORATE PHILOSOPHY AND FUNDING PRINCIPLES

Bankers Trust's guiding philosophy of "public responsibility and concern" recognizes a responsibility to the company's shareholders, customers, and employees and, at the same time, to the communities of the world in which it does business. This philosophy includes "a strong belief that the company's long-term prosperity depends on the quality of public institutions and the well-being of society and that helping people who lack opportunities or face great hardships is simply the ethical thing to do."[3] Management has defined a vision that calls on the company and its people to act as advocates for positive change, using their experience and skills both as professionals and as members of the global community. Page Chapman III, president of the Bankers Trust Foundation, explains, "We've given ourselves a mandate to truly become the 'corporate citizen' of the world. . . . That means more than just signing checks."[4] To this end, community development is a natural extension of Bankers Trust's philosophy. The company believes that, as a financial services firm, it can be most effective in using capital as its primary tool toward achieving self-sustaining communities and broadening opportunities for prosperity. It also places priority on the sustained involvement of the company's employees in community investment activities.

In the process of setting strategy and priorities, Chapman and the Foundation staff concluded that effective corporate citizenship required Bankers Trust to tightly focus its activities to ensure maximum benefit to both the community and the company itself. They also realized that their social responsibility activities had to be primarily shaped by strategic business goals and objectives. What evolved is a program guided by five fundamental principles: (1) to support collaborative ventures that bridge the interests and abilities of the private sector, governments, and local communities to define and implement projects that help meet the fundamental needs of poor people; (2) to build the capacity of the "third sector" (nonprofit/nongovernmental organizations) as a critical vehicle

3. From the Bankers Trust Foundation brochure, "Contributions Policy and Guidelines."

4. Interview with Chapman.

to advancing opportunities for distressed communities; (3) to foster the emergence of an entrepreneurial/business ownership class within low-income communities and to facilitate its access to credit; (4) to protect environmental resources as a means to achieve self-sustaining communities and economic growth; and (5) to enable the broadest access to quality education among disadvantaged people.[5]

An additional principle of Bankers Trust's corporate citizenship is the belief that a program should not just give money away but rather should incorporate a genuine partnership approach. The company should most appropriately rely on, and foster the development of, capable nongovernmental organizations (NGOs) as agents for change and as partners. Chapman notes, however, that the Foundation does not get involved in NGO-building itself. The Foundation must therefore rely on intermediary NGOs that are locally based and well qualified, making partnership formation a critical element of the Foundation's giving strategy.

IMPACT OF THE COMMUNITY REINVESTMENT ACT

In addition to fitting well with the Bankers Trust corporate philosophy, the choice of community development as a new focus was prompted by a second factor. In the 1960s and 1970s, banks started retreating from distressed inner-city communities en masse. This led the United States Congress to enact the Community Reinvestment Act (CRA) in 1977, which introduced a new set of regulations requiring financial institutions to continue offering banking services in poor communities and encouraging them to engage in activities to promote community revitalization within low- and moderate-income areas. Since Bankers Trust is a wholesale financial services firm rather than a commercial bank, and therefore has no branch banking facilities, senior company and Foundation executives decided that their method of giving back to the poor communities of New York City would be through grant making. Chapman admits that the CRA constituted the initial impetus for Bankers Trust to adopt community development as the new focus of its philanthropic giving. "If you do a good job, you get recognized by the government," which, as he added, was very important for a bank. "Good corporate citizenship is good business!"[6] Throughout most of the 1990s, Bankers Trust has earned "outstanding"

5. From the Bankers Trust Foundation brochure, "A Strategy for Global Corporate Citizenship."

6. Interview with Chapman.

CRA ratings from the Federal Reserve Bank of New York and the New York State Banking Department for its support to low- and moderate-income neighborhoods in New York City.

COLLABORATION WITH
THE LOCAL INITIATIVES SUPPORT CORPORATION

The initial and long-term partners in these domestic community development efforts have been the Local Initiatives Support Corporation (LISC) and local affiliate enterprises called Community Development Corporations (CDCs). Established by the Ford Foundation and six corporations in 1979, LISC is the nation's largest nonprofit community development support organization, and serves as a national intermediary that channels grants, investments, and technical support to CDCs that are rebuilding neighborhoods throughout the country.[7] CDCs are locally controlled nonprofit organizations that reinforce the economic and social foundation of neighborhoods and towns that are building their way out of years of disinvestment and decay. The CDCs create affordable homes for working families, spur commercial investment, create jobs, and expand opportunities in low-income neighborhoods.

From 1980 to 1987, the New York City LISC worked with CDCs to revitalize the devastated neighborhoods of the South Bronx. Building on the success there, it now works with groups in low- and moderate-income neighborhoods in the Bronx, Brooklyn, and Manhattan. Bankers Trust has formed a close partnership involving LISC, the New York City LISC and its affiliate CDCs, and the staff of the Foundation and Bankers Trust's Community Development Group.[8] One well-known success story is a neighborhood redevelopment project conducted by a CDC known as the Mid-Bronx Desperadoes, in which Bankers Trust took a special interest. Prior to the project's initiation, the area around Charlotte Gardens in the Bronx was a symbol of America's urban decay. Neighborhoods were burnt-out relics, abandoned by the middle class, torched by arsonists, and

7. LISC works in partnership with 1,900 corporations, foundations, public agencies (federal, state, and local), and increasing numbers of individual donors. To date, the organization has raised US$3 billion to support grass-roots community revitalization, 97 percent of which has come from private sources. CDCs have leveraged this money by raising an additional US$3.5 billion locally.

8. The Community Development Group is an arm of Bankers Trust that works closely with the Foundation in community development and offers low-interest loans, investment advice, and other financial services for community development.

plagued by drugs and crime. Driven by a vision of reconstructing their neighborhood as a resilient, economically diverse community, a coalition of concerned citizens representing community-based churches, tenant associations, and service organizations established the Mid-Bronx Desperadoes in 1974. The New York City LISC provided technical assistance on a daily basis, and more than US$210 million was raised from corporations and state, city, and federal funds. Bankers Trust, in addition to financial participation in the project, assigned its staff to work with project leaders. Twenty-three years later, in December 1997, President Bill Clinton visited the area to view the successful results of this public-private partnership. What he found was a reclaimed, clean, beautiful neighborhood, with new housing developments that offered thousands of affordable homes and apartments, and a health clinic for the neighborhood. The Mid-Bronx Desperadoes is also working to bring a major regional shopping center and small shops into the community to promote further economic development.

More recently, Bankers Trust's leadership has resulted in the creation of the Neighborhood 2000 Fund, a collaborative effort of 28 leading New York corporations and foundations that have provided more than US$10 million in support of CDCs rebuilding low-income neighborhoods throughout the city.[9] The Bankers Trust Foundation has spent some US$1.7 million annually in community development grants in recent years. In addition, the company itself has been investing several million dollars each year for this purpose in the form of grants and low-interest loans to LISC and CDCs through various innovative programs.

GOING INTERNATIONAL

In 1994, Bankers Trust embarked on an ambitious strategy to expand the reach of the Foundation beyond the United States to targeted communities in Asia, Latin America, and Europe. This globalization of the Foundation's philanthropic program mirrored the growth of the company's presence overseas and recognized the responsibility it had to serve as an active partner in the life of the diverse communities throughout the world in which Bankers Trust conducts business. Building on its successful domestic programs, community development became the focus for international programs as well. General priority was placed on projects that

9. Five of the 28 donors are Asian banks: Bank of China, Bank of Tokyo–Mitsubishi Trust, Fuji Bank and Trust, IBJ Foundation of Industrial Bank of Japan, and LTCB Trust.

sought to address common problems faced by poor neighborhoods in developing countries, as well as in megacities in the developed world, and to provide opportunities for self-reliance. Specific priorities, however, are established according to local needs, and funds support projects in which local Bankers Trust employees take an active role.

In Poland, Hungary, and the Czech Republic, for example, Bankers Trust Foundation has worked in partnership with the Soros Foundation to help foster the emergence of civil society and a viable nonprofit sector. In a number of Asian countries, the Foundation has supported comprehensive self-help approaches to reviving impoverished urban and rural villages. And in inner-city London, Bankers Trust support has helped to dramatically improve the academic performance of students. In 1998, approximately US$1 million of the Foundation's US$12 million budget was devoted to international giving.[10]

BANKERS TRUST'S COMMUNITY INVOLVEMENT IN ASIA

Bankers Trust has a long and active history of serving clients in the rapidly evolving markets of Asia Pacific, providing a hybrid of global and local expertise. The company has branch offices in most countries in Asia and a regional office located in Hong Kong. Each branch office provides wide-ranging financial services matching the specific needs of the country in which it operates, including corporate finance activities, trading and institutional services, and risk management advice. The Asian regional office in Hong Kong and the Japan branch in Tokyo have maintained a presence for more than 20 years and both have more than 300 employees.

Giving by the Bankers Trust Foundation in Asia Pacific began in 1994, the same year the Foundation's international program was established. That year, Bankers Trust opened its first China office in Beijing, and the head of the Asia regional office, who had extensive contacts in China, suggested that good corporate citizenship would be useful to gain goodwill and recognition in that country. Accordingly, the Foundation provided funding to a well-established NGO, the China Youth Development Foundation (CYDF), an independent, nonprofit social organization founded

10. The geographical distribution of giving by the Bankers Trust Foundation was US$400,000 for Europe, the Middle East, and Africa; US$200,000 for Latin America; and US$400,000 for Asia.

by the All-China Youth Federation in 1989 to promote the healthy development of Chinese youth and children. The announcement of the grant —the largest foreign gift CYDF had ever received—was made on June 15, 1994, during the opening ceremony of Bankers Trust's Beijing representative office. Bankers Trust committed US$575,000 over five years for the Community Development Fund for China, which would allow CYDF to build 25 primary schools in poverty-stricken areas of Hebei, Zhejiang, and Xinjing provinces. CYDF Chairman Yan Bingxuan accepted the donation on behalf of the organization, and Li Peiyao, vice chairman of the Standing Committee of the National People's Congress, issued a certificate of donation to Bankers Trust Foundation and expressed his thanks for its "righteous deed." The event was covered in the *People's Daily* and the national media, and continued to receive attention as the schools were completed. While this project was quite successful in terms of achieving its goals, and in terms of generating goodwill toward Bankers Trust in China, its one flaw was that it did not meet the normal standard of the Foundation for involving the company and its employees.

The following year, the Foundation expanded its international programs significantly, quadrupling its overall international budget from US$250,000 to US$1 million, and it began to work more actively in partnership with local organizations and governments in conducting community development. Among the projects that received support was an initiative undertaken by Bamlers Trust, its Thai affiliate, Thai Investment & Securities Co., and a business consortium, the Thai Business Initiative in Rural Development program, to help develop new farming techniques in three low-income villages. In Malaysia, where Bankers Trust opened a small office in 1995, the Foundation announced the formation of the Bankers Trust Community Development Fund for Malaysia, a US$200,000 commitment over four years to a governmental program that enabled the Malaysian business community to "adopt" disadvantaged communities throughout the country. In Singapore, Bankers Trust decided to team up with ENGENDER, a Singapore-based NGO dedicated to addressing issues related to the environment, gender, and development. They developed a novel project known as Sustainable Livelihoods through Craft Development, which provided employment for 40 low-income women in that country. Bankers Trust donated funds for this project, and company volunteers helped by providing materials and assisting with the marketing of the products. In Korea, 110 Bankers Trust employees formed a "Bankers Club," to foster a comprehensive redevelopment effort in a poor village outside of Seoul. This effort involved Bankers Trust, the employee-members of the Bankers Club, the leaders and citizens of the village, and a local NGO. And in Indonesia, Bankers Trust established a fund to provide two poor neighborhoods in the Jakarta area with access to training for small business start-ups.

As these examples illustrate, despite the relatively short history of the company's philanthropic involvement in the Asia Pacific region, Bankers Trust has made great strides in contributing to community development in Asia through the establishment of various models of corporate-NGO partnerships. In the view of the Foundation, however, perhaps the most successful model to date has been its work in the Philippines on the Barangay Improvement Project.

THE BARANGAY IMPROVEMENT PROJECT

PARTNERSHIP WITH PBSP
FOR COMMUNITY DEVELOPMENT

Bankers Trust enjoys a long history in the Philippines, having maintained an office there for nearly three decades. The Bankers Trust Foundation began making grants in the country in 1996, when it formed a partnership that Chapman believes turned out to be "an excellent model of the private sector, the public sector, and the third sector really getting together."[11] The project, formally named the Taguig Integrated Urban Estate Development Project—better known as the Barangay Improvement Project—was a community development project in an extremely poor neighborhood in Barangay Tipas of Taguig in Metro Manila.[12] To carry out the project, the Foundation worked together with PBSP, a corporate-sponsored organization that was the largest grant-making and project implementing foundation in the Philippines.

The idea for a partnership between Bankers Trust and PBSP began two years earlier, when Chapman met Aurora Tolentino, executive director of PBSP, and other Filipino business leaders at a 1994 Asia Pacific NGO conference sponsored by the Japan Center for International Exchange (JCIE) and at the ensuing Asia Pacific Philanthropy Consortium meeting in Osaka, Japan. Following those meetings, Bankers Trust became a member

11. Interview with Chapman.

12. The *barangay* represents the smallest unit of government in the Philippines, like a village or township.

of PBSP and continued to explore with it possible community development projects in the Philippines. PBSP's Board consists of prominent Filipino business leaders, many of whom the Bankers Trust Manila office either does business with or would like to, and the combination of PBSP's high profile and proven track record made it an attractive partner from Bankers Trust's perspective.

The first task was to choose the site for the project. As previously mentioned, Bankers Trust seeks to support projects in which its employees can become involved. Accordingly, when PBSP initially suggested several rural areas as potential locales, Bankers Trust Foundation pushed instead for sites closer to Metro Manila so that the company's local staff would be able to work as volunteers or advisors and be an integral part of the project. One prospective site in Barangay Tipas of Taguig drew the attention of Bankers Trust and PBSP. It seemed to symbolize the inner-city problems of Manila—"a city bursting at the seams, ringed by squatter housing settlements characterized by malnutrition, disease and few sources of potable water."[13] Though an impoverished neighborhood, the site was not hopeless, and it had a responsive community, as well as a homeowners association, the Bahayang Pag-asa ng Taguig Homeowners Association, Inc., with strong local leadership that welcomed the Foundation's investment. Chapman was impressed by the *barangay*'s spirit, and the Foundation decided in 1996 to commit US$80,000 over two years. A demonstration project was launched to target the area for comprehensive improvement.

AYALA JOINS TO FORM TRIPARTITE PARTNERSHIP

Central to the effort in Barangay Tipas was capacity building, or empowerment of residents, to make the community self-reliant. During the process of working with PBSP in planning the project, Bankers Trust Foundation decided to invite another intermediary partner to handle the job training aspect. The Foundation asked the Ayala Foundation, Inc., to join the project as a co-partner. Chapman had met the Ayala executive director, Victoria Garchitorena, at the 1994 JCIE conference, and the Ayala family is also an important client of Bankers Trust, so a connection between the organizations already existed. The Foundation committed an additional US$20,000 to Ayala for the job training program for the local villagers, bringing its total commitment to the project to US$100,000.

13. From a Bankers Trust publication, "Global Reach: Building a Global Village," p. 9.

PROJECT IMPLEMENTATION AND ACCOMPLISHMENTS

The Barangay Improvement Project began in February 1996. It was a post–land acquisition project that was designed to "transform the lives of once landless/homeless urban poor families into productive, secure and self-reliant citizens."[14] At the outset of the project, the site was a microcosm of the inner-city poverty problem in the Philippines today. This area was prone to flooding and had no drainage or road system. The community was not organized and there was insufficient delivery of basic social services. The project components therefore included community organizing and capacity building, including job training, daycare assistance, and livelihood development, and the development of infrastructure such as roads, water drainage, and sanitation facilities. This integrated approach proved effective in achieving resettlement on the site. The project also stressed the participation of and partnership with people in the community through the entire process of planning, decision making, and project implementation. This strategy not only insured the smooth execution of the project but also motivated the residents to be more cooperative and accountable.

PBSP provided overall technical assistance to the homeowners association and at the same time assigned a project manager who was involved on a daily basis on the site, serving as a liaison for the village leaders and the informal community group. The Ayala Foundation provided job and skills training, particularly in cooperative development and management, and in livelihood development primarily for housewives. Training was offered in such areas as the floral business, meat processing, slipper making, dress making, and cosmetology. Ayala provided loan assistance to create small, home-based businesses, while the local government of Taguig and businesses also provided various forms of assistance and services.

The local Bankers Trust staff—from the clerical staff to the middle management and the country head—visited the site once every four to six weeks to advise the villagers and help with business plans. Chapman himself made several visits to observe the progress. With PBSP's technical assistance, villagers built new roads and other infrastructure on their own. One of the major roads was named Bankers Trust Avenue as a symbol of the community's appreciation for the company's generosity and involvement in urban poverty alleviation initiatives in the Philippines.

14. From PBSP's "Terminal Report of the 'Taguig Integrated Urban Estate Development Project,'" presented to the Bankers Trust Foundation, February 1998.

The project presented a case in which donor organizations graduated "from just a financial donor to a more strategic position of partnership with the community," according to the final PBSP project report. The report noted that the consultations, frequent visits, and presence of Bankers Trust representatives and other organizations both provided business advice and guidance and "boosted the morale of the community."

"DREAM PARTNERSHIP" ACCOMPLISHES MISSION

The PBSP final report to Bankers Trust Foundation summarized the project results. In terms of human resource development and organizational building, the project improved the capacities of community organizations to manage projects and to run local development affairs. The project also provided much-needed infrastructure development and such basic social services as daycare assistance, supplemental parental care, and other health care assistance. Moreover, the project offered poverty alleviation opportunities through the establishment of micro-enterprises and through livelihood development and skills training. As a result, the project was able to achieve its objective of "transforming the lives of the once landless urban poor into productive and self-reliant citizens."[15] The project directly benefited 138 households of Barangay Tipas. The village is now "self-sustained," and people on the site have developed a sense of "ownership"—a very important emphasis of Bankers Trust giving, as pointed out by Chapman. Indeed, the Barangay Improvement Project is a good example of Bankers Trust Foundation's corporate-NGO partnership strategy—the project involved the company's local staff and clients, NGOs, local corporate givers, the community itself, and the local government of Taguig, making it a truly multilateral partnership.

Chapman noted that despite all the success of the Barangay Improvement Project, his one frustration was that only 138 families were beneficiaries. He thought this number was too small given the vast needs in Metro Manila. One hopeful outcome, however, is a follow-up project in another site in Metro Manila, Barangay Project II, which got under way in October 1998. This new two-year project is once again jointly initiated by the Bankers Trust Foundation, PBSP, and the Ayala Foundation, in partnership with the local government of Barangay Ibayo. The Foundation is again providing funding in the amount of US$100,000 (US$80,000 for PBSP and US$20,000 for Ayala), but this new effort is much larger in scale

15. Ibid.

than the first project and is expected to benefit more than 2,000 poor urban families.

REQUIREMENTS FOR
SUCCESSFUL NGO PARTNERSHIPS

From its experiences with a variety of NGO partnerships, Bankers Trust Foundation has identified a number of prerequisites for a successful corporate-NGO partnership. First, Chapman stressed the need to localize the projects. Working with local NGOs and involving the company's local staff or local affiliates—given their familiarity with local needs, language, society, and culture—is critical for the success of any international project the Foundation supports. In addition, local leadership must be central to all efforts, and the "ownership" of projects must lie with the community. Those in the private sector (companies and corporate foundations), as well as those in government, are best suited to the role of the "enabler," providing support to indigenous ambitions.

A second important lesson is that government needs to recognize the value of its involvement in helping to mitigate risks for corporate involvement. In most instances, the government, as the provider of the most significant resources, can facilitate cooperative efforts or can block them through impenetrable bureaucracy. Communities and governments need to understand the motivations for corporate citizenship and should foster relationships that address these needs.

Third, it is important to understand that the working culture of the private sector, which tends to be result oriented, is different than that of government and communities, which are more process oriented. Each partner therefore needs to recognize these differences and seek common ground. NGOs in Asia, in particular, need to learn to be more result-oriented, and Bankers Trust Foundation is trying to help its NGO partners in this respect by advising them on how to set goals, devise strategies, and make business plans. Corporations, for their part, must bear in mind that community development tends by nature to be process oriented. At Bankers Trust, Chapman notes, "We often need to remind ourselves that we are not working toward the consummation of a particular deal but rather we are investing in long-term partnerships, the development of individual leaders and the capacity of entire communities."[16] These outcomes

16. Interview with Chapman.

cannot be measured at the end of a quarter in the same manner as a company's financial performance.

Because differences do exist in context and culture, partner organizations must clearly define the motivation for their involvement as well as the expected outcomes of any partnership. Expectations need to be grounded in the reality of the difficulty of the tasks at hand.

Finally, according to Chapman, Bankers Trust Foundation places a special emphasis on the monitoring and evaluation of its programs. To effectively and meaningfully address fundamental human needs through corporate citizenship can seem an overwhelming and insurmountable challenge. Indeed, the fear of failure can be the primary justification for corporate inaction. For these reasons, it is essential to monitor and evaluate the benefits and outcomes of corporate citizenship.

CONCLUSION

The descriptions and examples of philanthropic activities presented in the preceding sections illustrate the content and quality of Bankers Trust's role as a global corporate citizen. The benefits derived by Bankers Trust from these activities are numerous. The company can articulate and represent its core values. It can reflect and reinforce the character of the company as a truly global institution through local commitments that respond to country-specific needs and priorities. It provides opportunities for employees to actively participate in and lead community development projects, thus broadening their skills set and enabling them to showcase their abilities to senior management. Community partnerships have also enabled Bankers Trust representatives to network with other business leaders, government officials, and prospective clients outside of the usual business forums. And ultimately, political and economic stability, nurtured by a civil society committed to social and economic justice, bodes well for Bankers Trust's long-term business interests.

As countries in Asia Pacific strive to reform and revitalize themselves through political and economic renewal, the efforts of civil society will be essential, and will need to be further developed. In this context, it is hoped that Bankers Trusst will continue its philanthropic activities in the region, and that it will serve as an example for other corporations in the United States and Asia, encouraging them to forge corporate-NGO partnerships that can contribute to the social stability of tomorrow's Asia Pacific.

8 Levi Strauss Donor Advised Fund in Japan

Hideko Katsumata
and
Susan Hubbard

THE brand name Levi Strauss & Co. is among the most recognized in the United States and around the world. Even those who do not know the name are likely to be familiar with the company's denim blue jeans with the double-arch stitch on the back pocket. Each pair of Levi's® blue jeans bears a leather patch with the words "Original Riveted Clothing" and the date May 20, 1873—the historic date when the company first used metal rivets on its clothing. Levi Strauss & Co. is one of the oldest apparel manufacturers in the United States. Its founder, Levi Strauss, moved to San Francisco during the Gold Rush and established a company that produced durable clothing to meet the demands of the miners. With the slogan "Quality never goes out of style," the company has grown to be one of the largest apparel manufacturers in the world.

Still headquartered in San Francisco, Levi Strauss & Co. is also well known to many in California and elsewhere in the United States for its corporate philanthropy and community involvement activities. The company donates 2.5 percent of pretax earnings annually—a total of US$22 million in 1998—and is recognized for its leading role in enhancing AIDS awareness and prevention, and for Project Change, an antiracism initiative of the Levi Strauss Foundation. And while charity may begin at home, as they say, Levi Strauss has been generous overseas as well. As its business operations have expanded globally, the company's international philanthropic activities have also grown, topping US$7 million in 1998. This chapter examines the corporate philosophy of Levi Strauss & Co., which emphasizes community involvement as an integral element of its philanthropy, and focuses on some of the efforts that the company has exerted in applying its corporate philosophy in the diverse sociocultural and political environments of Asian countries.

LEVI STRAUSS & CO.'S PHILOSOPHY OF CORPORATE PHILANTHROPY AND COMMUNITY INVOLVEMENT

A FAMILY TRADITION

Levi Strauss & Co. is a family-owned corporation that has inherited a long family tradition of philanthropic giving. Levi Strauss's heirs have set up numerous private foundations, the total assets of which exceed US$1 billion. The Haas family of San Francisco inherited and still runs the blue jeans company. The philanthropic tradition of the family was mainly established by Walter Haas, Sr., who married the daughter of one of Levi Strauss's nephews and who ran the company from 1928 to 1955. Robert D. Haas, the current chairman of the board and chief executive officer, is the grandson of Walter Haas, Sr., and is following in his grandfather's charitable footsteps. He was a trustee of the Ford Foundation, serves on the boards of many nonprofit organizations, and is well known as a leading figure in the philanthropic community in the United States and around the world. Not only did Robert Haas bring the company's revenue to US$7.1 billion in 1996, making it the world's largest apparel manufacturer at the time, but he also strengthened the philanthropic tradition within the company.

Speaking to a 1996 Keidanren (Japan Federation of Economic Organizations) Study Mission on Corporate-NGO Partnership, Robert Haas discussed his family's tradition of philanthropy and good corporate citizenship, explaining that the founder, Levi Strauss, "believed in high-quality products, fair prices, and a strong commitment to the community. He established our company's strong tradition of corporate social responsibility that continues to this day. Levi Strauss believed in giving back to the community because it was the right thing to do. It also turned out to be good for business."

EMPHASIZING VALUES AND COMMUNITY

To reinforce the company's commitment to the community, Levi Strauss & Co. adopted a mission and aspiration statement that asserts, "We will conduct our business ethically and demonstrate leadership in satisfying our responsibilities to our communities and the society." The translation of such a noble goal into practical business behavior, however, is a constant challenge. As Robert Haas admitted in a Conference Board speech in 1994, "We at Levi Strauss & Co. struggle every day with how to create a business culture that promotes ethical behavior." Eschewing the "compliance-based approach" of rules and regulations, Levi Strauss & Co. has instead opted for a "values-oriented approach" that emphasizes six ethical principles: honesty, promise keeping, fairness, respect for others, compassion, and integrity. These principles are applied both internally in the daily management of the company and externally in the relationship between Levi Strauss & Co. and the community.

Haas also emphasized in his speech that "there is a positive correlation between good corporate citizenship and financial performance," citing recent studies that underscored the point "that companies which look beyond solely maximizing wealth and profits and are driven by values and a sense of purpose outperform those companies that focus only on short-term gain." Other recent studies suggest, according to Haas, that "how a company conducts itself affects consumer purchasing decisions and customer loyalty."

Levi Strauss & Co.'s promotion of good corporate citizenship has been primarily oriented toward the well-being of communities in which its employees live and work. Again, Robert Haas stated in his speech to the Keidanren mission that "my great-great granduncle had a vision of how companies should relate to their communities. He envisioned a company that could be a financial success while acting as a powerful force for social change." With this goal in mind, Levi Strauss & Co. has developed a number of innovative methods for its employees to contribute to their communities, both in the United States and overseas, by donating money, time, and expertise.

THE LEVI STRAUSS FOUNDATION

Levi Strauss & Co.'s philanthropic activities are conducted through the corporation itself and through the Levi Strauss Foundation. Created in 1952 to ensure the stability of the company's philanthropic programs, the Foundation is responsible for programs in the United States, while the corporation is responsible for overseas programs. An endowment was set up for the Foundation by Levi Strauss & Co. to insulate it from fluctuations in business performance. The Foundation is governed by a board, and daily operations are conducted by the staff members of the corporation's Global Public Affairs Department.

COMMUNITY-BASED SOCIAL RESPONSIBILITY PROGRAMS WITH NGO PARTNERSHIP

Levi Strauss & Co. has developed a multipronged approach to community involvement, placing a strong emphasis on employee participation and on partnership with nongovernmental organizations (NGOs) working in the communities where the company operates. Under the heading of "community partnership programs," the Levi Strauss Foundation channels its resources primarily to three programs: the Community Involvement Team (CIT) Program, the Community Partnership Program, and Employee Giving Programs. CIT and employee giving activities are identified and decided upon by the employees themselves and reflect the needs that they perceive in their communities. Community partnership programs in the United States are determined by the Foundation; in other countries, decisions regarding funding are made by the community affairs managers in the respective regional headquarters.

To encourage employees in the United States to be active in their communities, employees are given ample information about philanthropic and partnership activities and outcomes, and are provided with office space for coordinating CIT activities during their lunch hour. Incentives come in the form of encouragement and support from the corporation and the opportunity to choose the kind of work they will do to help improve their communities. Employee involvement and financial support seem to be emphasized equally. Employee involvement also entails educating employees about social issues. One important aspect of an AIDS prevention and care project in San Francisco, for example, involved educating employees about AIDS prevention and about how to deal with friends, family members, and fellow employees who are HIV positive.

COMMUNITY PARTNERSHIP PROGRAMS

Levi Strauss & Co. and the Levi Strauss Foundation provide financial assistance to NGOs for projects in four general areas: community-based economic development, AIDS prevention and care, social justice, and youth empowerment. These priority areas are modified to respond to changing social needs, with youth empowerment being added only in 1997.

The company has received accolades for its leading role in promoting AIDS awareness and prevention, which began at the initiative of a group of employees. According to Haas, the employees approached the company's senior management in 1982 to seek their endorsement for distribution of literature on this new disease that was suddenly taking an alarming toll on so many communities in the United States, and particularly in San Francisco. Haas and senior managers joined the employees in staffing a booth and distributing literature to other Levi Strauss & Co. employees, many of whom frowned upon such activities at the time because of a lack of knowledge about the disease. Since that time, the company has made AIDS prevention and care one of its top priorities in communities around the world, and since 1983 has contributed more than US$2 million in grants for assistance to AIDS patients and their caregivers, risk reduction education, and services targeted at populations severely affected by AIDS.

Because many of the communities where Levi Strauss & Co. employees reside are in need of increased economic opportunities, the company also works closely with NGOs that promote programs focused on job creation and community-based economic development, as well as micro-enterprise development schemes. At the same time, community-based economic development grants are provided for the purpose of leadership development, thus strengthening the economic development capacity of community organizations and their leaders.

COMMUNITY INVOLVEMENT TEAM PROGRAM

To enhance employee involvement in the company's social responsibility activities, Levi Strauss & Co. devised a unique mechanism known as Community Involvement Teams (CITs). In 1968, the first Community Affairs Department was created to organize workers throughout the company into groups of volunteers, offering them start-up money and matching the groups' own fund-raising efforts. Since then, 100 CITs have been formed around the world.

The CITs are groups of employees from all levels of the corporation who volunteer their time and services to organizations of their choice. They are allocated some of the community affairs budget to manage themselves in connection with their volunteer work. The CITs are free to carry out their activities as they see fit within the broad guidelines set out by the corporation, and while the CITs are granted considerable autonomy, they often approach the corporation for guidance, advice, and technical assistance. These groups of volunteers not only provide a service to their communities but also gain fund-raising and community development experience themselves.

EMPLOYEE GIVING PROGRAMS

Levi Strauss & Co. encourages employees to contribute financially to their communities through three types of employee giving programs. The first type is a matching gifts program, through which the Foundation will give up to US$1,200 annually per employee for qualified community organizations and educational programs. The second type is community service grants, through which the Foundation makes grants of up to US$600 for organizations where Levi Strauss & Co. employees volunteer their time. The third type is workplace giving, through which the Foundation cooperates with United Way and other approved nonprofit organizations to coordinate giving.

COMMUNITY INVOLVEMENT IN ASIA PACIFIC

As Levi Strauss & Co. started expanding its operations worldwide, it decided to decentralize its corporate philanthropic activities to better "think globally, act locally," as the saying goes. This decentralization has evolved along with the growth of the company's business, starting in Europe, then North and South America, and then Asia Pacific. To ensure that the giving is responsive to the local communities, each region is assigned a local public affairs director. The budget allocation to individual countries within the region is based on needs and opportunities in those countries.

As one strategy, Levi Strauss Foundation decided to adopt an ambitious new approach to localizing its community involvement activities by initiating "donor advised funds." As will be discussed in greater detail below, a donor advised fund (DAF) is comprised of a grant made to a nonprofit organization, which in turn makes grants to other beneficiaries. Through the grant, the donor has the authority to advise the grantee institution regarding the distribution of the DAF grants, although donees are free to disregard the advice of the donor. This new type of grant is currently being conducted on an experimental basis in Japan with the Japan Center for International Exchange (JCIE) and in France with the Fondation de France.

Whether it be through DAF grants or direct funding, the four priority areas of the overall philanthropic activities of the company are followed in each region and country, although a limited number of "off-guidelines" grants are provided, usually for urgent issues such as disaster relief, or in special cases where Levi Strauss & Co. sees an opportunity to play a major leadership role in bringing an important issue into focus in a given community.

There are also regionwide projects—about 10 percent of the annual giving in the Asia Pacific region—that do not focus on a single community but rather encourage regional information sharing or community building. One such example is a grant to the AIDS Society of the Philippines to plan and organize regional skills-building workshops to share knowledge and best practices among HIV/AIDS prevention agencies in the Asia Pacific region.

As is the case in the United States, corporate-NGO partnerships in Asia are promoted by Community Involvement Teams. For example, a CIT in Levi Strauss Philippines identified a handicraft producers cooperative that could receive donations of denim scraps, unused labels, and zippers—waste that would normally be sent to a landfill. The cooperative in turn hired local people to manufacture such small mementos as Levi's® pencil cases, book bags, and bookmarks. Levi Strauss Philippines purchased these handicrafts, thus supporting local employment. Finally, Levi Strauss Philippines distributed the handicrafts in its stores to promote the sale of Levi's® jeans. This collaboration was a win-win situation for the NGO, the environment, and the business.

While these community activities have been largely successful, Levi Strauss & Co. has encountered some serious challenges in applying its corporate philosophy to its business operations in different sociocultural environments. In 1992, Levi Strauss & Co. was the first company to launch a corporate code of conduct governing the responsible manufacturing of its products in contractor facilities. In Bangladesh, Levi Strauss & Co. representatives discovered that its contractor was employing children in violation of the company's global sourcing guidelines. Rather than force the contractor to let the children go, which would likely lead to those children taking up prostitution or more dangerous work, Levi Strauss & Co. convinced the contractor to take them off the sewing lines and continue to pay them their wages. The contractor and Levi Strauss & Co. worked together to identify a local school that would accept the children. While the contractor continued their wages, Levi Strauss & Co. paid for the school fees, books, and uniforms so the children could attend school.

The contractor agreed to offer jobs to the children upon graduation from school. The contractor also agreed not to hire any more child labor. This innovative solution has become a national trade model for the garment industry. In addition, the Levi Strauss Foundation provided funding for the start-up of a joint project with UNICEF, the Bangladesh Garment and Manufacturers and Exporters Association, and the International Labor Organization, which is ensuring that underage factory workers are able to attend school while receiving stipends to support themselves and their families. This NGO partnership has proven to be a useful tool for creating effective solutions that address the challenges in the Bangladesh garment industry.

THE CASE OF JAPAN

GENESIS OF JCIE'S ASSOCIATION WITH LEVI STRAUSS & CO.

JCIE began its association with Levi Strauss & Co. more than a decade ago. In early 1986, JCIE had offered to arrange a study mission to Asia for a delegation of Foundation representatives from the West Coast of the United States. Ultimately, the program did not materialize, but one individual who had shown great interest in joining the mission was Martha Montag Brown, then manager of Community Affairs and Contributions at Levi Strauss & Co. Later that same year, she paid a visit to Japan to raise awareness about employee volunteerism within Levi Strauss Japan. At that time, corporate philanthropy was a completely new concept in Japan, and although there were some signs of the emergence of NGOs in Japanese society, it was almost impossible to find employees from Japanese corporations doing volunteer work. Prior to making that trip, Montag Brown wrote to Tadashi Yamamoto, president of JCIE, asking if he would organize meetings for her with Japanese foundations while she was in the country. Since that time, JCIE has worked closely with Levi Strauss & Co.

In 1988, JCIE organized the Study Mission on Good Corporate Citizenship in the United States with Keidanren and brought managers of corporate contributions from major business corporations and associations to Levi Strauss & Co. headquarters among other sites in San Francisco, New York, Washington, D.C., and Minneapolis/St. Paul. This mission inspired the Japanese delegates, and consequently JCIE and Keidanren organized an international symposium on "Becoming Good

Corporate Citizens in American Communities: New Challenges for Japanese Corporations in an Interdependent World" in November 1989. Michael Howard, president of the Asia Pacific Division of Levi Strauss International, was invited to be a speaker at this symposium. Since then, JCIE has organized programs whenever members of Levi Strauss & Co. visit Japan and has introduced them to Japanese businesses and NGOs interested in corporate philanthropy.

In 1997, relations between Levi Strauss & Co. and JCIE entered a new phase. In early February, Hideko Katsumata, executive secretary of JCIE, received a telephone call from Community Affairs at Levi Strauss & Co. headquarters, inquiring whether JCIE would be interested in becoming the agent for the Levi Strauss Foundation partnership program in Japan.

DONOR ADVISED FUND

After a series of meetings, correspondence, and international telephone conferences, the Levi Strauss Foundation and JCIE agreed in 1997 to start with an experimental grant in the amount of US$160,000, referred to as a donor advised fund. This grant was given to JCIE to redistribute to NGOs in Japan according to general guidelines set by the Levi Strauss Foundation. In a DAF, the relationship between the donor and donee is one in which the donor advises the donee on grant decisions.

JCIE recognized the unique opportunity this fund would provide for the nonprofit sector in Japan. It plays an important role by (1) supporting the institution-building of organizations in their initial stages; (2) providing flexibility in managing and financing a group's activities, as the grant will be provided at the outset of the project (many Japanese sources will grant money only after the project is successfully completed and the necessary financial documents are submitted); (3) considering applications to cope with emerging issues not yet well recognized in the community.

Once the DAF funds had been committed, JCIE called for grant applications in Levi Strauss & Co.'s four designated priority areas. By tapping its network of small grass-roots organizations active in these areas, JCIE received 50 applications within a month, of which 22 organizations received grants totaling US$160,000. The second year, 59 applications were received, and 24 organizations divided the US$160,000 fund. Grants have included support for the Asian People's Friendship Society to protect and improve the rights of foreigners in Japan who have overstayed their visas, and funding for Palette, an NGO that provides a place for mentally challenged people to meet, work, and live as part of the community.

CIT ACTIVITIES AT LEVI STRAUSS JAPAN

Levi Strauss & Co.'s first Japan branch office was established in 1971, and in 1982 Levi Strauss Japan K.K. was incorporated with capital of ¥3.78 billion (U.S.$32.6 million at ¥115.70 = US$1). The CIT was created in Japan three years later, formed from the staff of the Personnel Department, for whom it was half volunteer, half assigned work.

Ken'ichi Ogiwara, who joined Levi Japan's accounting department in 1990, was instrumental in transforming the CIT into a more active entity. He had been active in volunteer activities before he joined Levi Strauss Japan, and soon was able to encourage all the departments to join the CIT, with at least one person participating from each section. The 20-member team decided that it should become more proactive in finding grantees instead of relying on recommendations from an outside NGO. They also encouraged employee volunteerism and started advertising opportunities for volunteer work. At that time, while American executives were sympathetic toward their activities, the Japanese executives were less receptive. Nonetheless, CIT members started to take action, joining a project to bring physically challenged children to Disneyland; holding bazaars within the company to raise funds for their activities; joining charity marathons; and so on. Their work began to be recognized, and eventually they were even able to secure two pages on corporate philanthropy and community involvement in their company brochures.

The second phase of the CIT was to go out and find grant recipients, and they began their search by visiting the Social Welfare Association of Minato Ward, where they were received with puzzlement: Why was a foreign company interested in supporting minor grass-roots organizations? Even the grass-roots organizations themselves had difficulty believing that Levi Strauss Japan was sincere in its desire to support such activities. But Ogiwara visited most of the organizations that the Levi Strauss Japan CIT was supporting and established a relationship with them.

CHALLENGES FOR THE CIT MEMBERS

The major challenge, as Ogiwara points out, has been to change the perception of people both within and outside the company and recruit them to join in the action. When the company was enjoying the fruits of the "bubble" economy, it had substantial funding and could expand its activities. However, after the bubble burst, corporate restructuring led to increased workloads and greater demands on the employees' time, leaving little time to spare for the extra work of volunteering. Participation in the CIT activities diminished at the same time as demands to support community activities dramatically increased. After the Great Hanshin-Awaji Earthquake in Kobe, Japanese civil society began to emerge on a new scale, addressing a broad range of social issues such as domestic violence, child abuse, anti–land mine campaigns, revitalization of the community, and other social welfare issues. Accordingly, Levi Strauss Japan had to find a new way to cope with the new challenges facing Japanese society.

In response, the Levi Strauss & Co. headquarters suggested a partnership with JCIE. This led to heated arguments among CIT members over the question of whether they should depend on an outside NGO, but Ogiwara persuaded them that such a strategy was necessary given the current limitations. He also realized that working with a third party would provide an objective perspective that would be helpful since he himself tended to become so deeply involved and committed to each recipient organization. The members eventually accepted this proposition and started to work with JCIE.

CHALLENGES FOR JCIE

One major challenge for JCIE was to be sensitive to the aspirations and enthusiasm that had been cultivated among the members of the CIT. Although JCIE bears the ultimate responsibility in redistributing the DAF grants, it has tried to invite members of the CIT to participate in the process, as well as in the final screening of the grant applications. After the first year, some members of the CIT confessed to Ogiwara that they realized they had much to learn about managing grant-making activities, and that they wanted to continue to learn from this partnership so that they would be able to operate at the same level as a professional NGO in the future. These were encouraging words for JCIE.

Another challenge for JCIE has been to grasp the overall picture of the fields that the Levi Strauss Foundation wishes to support and to reach out to needy grass-roots organizations. It certainly has given JCIE the opportunity to expand its scope and learn about citizens' activities at the grass-roots level, adding to its understanding of current social issues as well.

As forerunners of a new type of working relationship—the donor advised fund—JCIE and Levi Strauss Foundation must also challenge themselves to find appropriate ways of encouraging other Japanese businesses to find creative and innovative ways of pursuing corporate-NGO partnerships.

CONCLUSION

Levi Strauss & Co. regards the donor advised funds in Japan and France to be successful, and is exploring similar arrangements in other countries. The Levi Strauss Foundation staff has noted a number of advantages to this new model of community involvement. First, the DAF enables the company to leverage in-country expertise and, based on shared values and funding interests, develop a strong partnership with the intermediary organization. Second, forging links between grass-roots NGOs and local, established intermediaries contributes to strengthening the nonprofit sector overall. Third, by choosing a strong and well-respected intermediary with links to in-country stakeholders, the company's grant making can receive a higher profile by association. Fourth, funds for evaluation, administration, and other staffing tasks are treated as part of the grant, thereby relieving corporate operating budgets and allowing funds to be redirected to support grant-making activities in other countries. (Obviously, the merit of such cost saving should be carefully reviewed, as the staff time and costs associated with the DAF model, such as coordinating employee advisory committees, managing fund relationships, and legal fees to set them up, can be substantial.) Fifth, because there is basically one "grantee," or one conduit that the employees now deal with in each country, the staff workload and the logistical and linguistic issues have been reduced.

For the intermediary NGOs that serve as the grantees of the donor advised funds, this model allows them to respond to what they judge to be the priority concerns in the NGO community in their country, which in turn can satisfy Levi Strauss & Co.'s desire to respond to stakeholders' interests. JCIE, in fact, has expanded its network and improved its staff's capacity to work with NGOs in Japan, which in turn should make JCIE better equipped to respond to Levi Strauss & Co.'s interests.

Bearing these points in mind, there seem to be several requirements for creating a successful partnership between donor and intermediary in a DAF. First, the donor and the intermediary should share a similar grant-making philosophy, goals, and values in order to foster mutual trust and a collegial spirit. Second, there should be close communication between the two organizations so as to share information on grant opportunities and to ensure that the grants match the donor's interests. Third, because it is the intermediary organization that issues the grant checks, that organization should make sure that full credit for the grants be given to the donor, so that individual grantees can establish a relationship with the donor or its local affiliate. Fourth, and related to the third, the intermediary should make every effort to involve local staff of the donor in the grant-making activities. Unless these factors are sufficiently emphasized, the original intention of the donor, in this case the Levi Strauss Foundation, to effectively implement its basic philosophy of corporate community involvement in foreign countries will not be realized.

9 Toyota Able Art Forum

Mio Kawashima

AROUND the world, the name Toyota is synonymous with automobiles. Since its establishment in 1937, Toyota Motor Corporation has grown to be the leading automobile manufacturer in Japan and one of the top three automakers worldwide. The company attributes its strength not only to the quality of its cars but also to its efforts to fulfill its role as a responsible corporate citizen.

Toyota was one of the pioneers of corporate philanthropy in Japan. During the era of high economic growth, when the entire country was focused on industrial development, most Japanese companies placed little importance on philanthropy. Toyota, however, recognized the value of corporate involvement in activities not motivated by profit and early on became active in the local communities where it operates. While many other Japanese companies are today just starting to understand the importance of community involvement activities, Toyota already has a well-established structure for exercising corporate philanthropy and conducts successful programs in Japan and abroad.

Recently, Toyota's philanthropic efforts entered a new stage in which the company works in partnership with nongovernmental organizations (NGOs) to undertake community involvement projects. One such partnership is the Toyota Able Art Forum, a project to promote arts by the disabled, which Toyota conducts in collaboration with the nonprofit Association of Art, Culture, and People with Disabilities. In addition to drawing on the strengths of these two organizations, the project has also successfully mobilized individuals from local communities and local governments by forming executive committees to run the Toyota Able Art Forum in various cities across Japan.

TOYOTA MOTOR CORPORATION

Toyota's wide spectrum of businesses includes the manufacturing of automobiles and automotive parts, industrial equipment, and prefabricated housing. Toyota heads a group of 233 subsidiaries and 149 affiliated companies worldwide, and the group's consolidated annual sales far outperform its competitors in the domestic market. Toyota also holds a competitive position in overseas markets. The company currently has production sites in 24 countries and 107 subsidiaries in 30 countries and regions.

TOYOTA'S CORPORATE PHILOSOPHY

Although Toyota is a publicly listed company, the influence of the founding Toyoda family remains strong, and the philosophy of the original founder, Sakichi Toyoda, still imbues the company's corporate philosophy today.[1] Since its establishment, Toyota has committed itself "to serve the community through manufacturing automobiles," and has adhered to the traditional policy of "customers first."[2] Accordingly, the company measures its success by its ability to satisfy its customers in every aspect of its activities—whether that be manufacturing, service, or community involvement.

This philosophy is evident in the seven "guiding principles" that Toyota established for its corporate activities in 1992 (and subsequently revised in 1997). These principles reflect the company's character as an "international corporation and a good corporate citizen that puts people, society, and the environment first and foremost."[3] That spirit was also captured in the company slogan announced in 1996, "Vision Theme for 2005," which focused on "harmonious growth." This vision for the next decade

---

1. Sakichi Toyoda invented a weaving machine, which was the start of the Toyota machinery business. His son, Kiichiro Toyoda, founded the Toyota Motor Corporation in 1937.

2. "Corporate Values That Create Brand Equities," *Brain* (May 1998), p. 36.

3. Toyota Web site < http://www.toyota.co.jp/e/pr/1997/0401.html > (December 1998).

stressed harmony with the global environment, with the global economy, with the company's various stakeholders (e.g., customers, shareholders, and employees), and with the local communities in which the company operates.

Toyota's view of community involvement is one of enlightened self-interest. A 1990 Toyota publication on public-interest activities, for example, notes that the company's philanthropic activities "can help earn a welcome place in the communities we serve through good corporate citizenship. And that will contribute to our growth over the long term."[4] Thus, while Toyota does not believe in publicizing its philanthropic activities as a marketing strategy, stressing that community involvement activities should be undertaken for purer motives, the company acknowledges that these activities help foster the name recognition so critical in the automobile industry. Especially in the American and European markets, good corporate citizenship is one element that is thought to have contributed to the company's success.

SUPPORT STRUCTURE FOR TOYOTA'S PHILANTHROPY

In the belief that meaningful and efficient community involvement activities "demand an organizational commitment as well as a financial one," Toyota has sought to involve top management in its philanthropic decision-making process.[5] In 1989, the Social Contribution Committee was established at Toyota's Tokyo headquarters, chaired by the president himself and comprised of the directors of the various philanthropy-related departments of Toyota. The committee determines the priority areas and budget for activities and plans the overall coordination of various projects. The largest committee within the company, it meets twice a year with the president, vice presidents, and all related division directors, showing a high degree of commitment among the top-level management to corporate philanthropy and to community involvement activities.

The Social Contribution Committee works closely with a number of divisions and departments in the company, but those primarily responsible for Toyota's various philanthropic activities are the Public Affairs Division, the General Affairs Division, and the Government Relations

4. *Neighbors* (December 1990), p. 2.

5. Ibid., p. 4.

Division. The Public Affairs Division oversees the company's commit-ment to arts and culture and to the environment. The Corporate Citi-zenship Department is a part of this division that focuses specifically on Toyota's activities in the field of arts and culture.[6] The General Affairs Di-vision promotes science- and technology-related programs, but its main task is to coordinate Toyota's overall philanthropic activities. It also oversees the Toyota Volunteer Center, which was established in 1993 to encourage and enhance employee involvement in various philanthropic activities. The Government Relations Division is responsible for oversee-ing some of Toyota's philanthropic and community involvement activi-ties overseas, as is the Public Affairs Division.

Toyota has conducted community involvement activities abroad since the 1980s, seeking to meet the various needs of the local communities in which it operates and to make the company more accessible to its host communities. These efforts, usually focused on the fields of education and environment, have contributed somewhat to easing the negative at-titudes toward Japanese companies that resulted from trade frictions. Although the underlying direction, principles, and priority areas are co-ordinated out of the headquarters in Japan through the Government and Industrial Affairs Division, the individual projects and their contents are determined by the local Toyota subsidiaries. Some local subsidiaries have also chosen to establish their own corporate foundations.

Apart from these activities, the company established the Toyota Foun-dation in 1974, which funds research and other projects in Japan and Southeast Asia in a variety of fields, such as civil society, the living and natural environments, social welfare, education, and culture. Although the Foundation receives funding from the parent company, its activities and operations are totally independent from the community involvement activities of Toyota Motor Corporation and from the parent company's corporate philosophy and strategy.

THE SCOPE OF TOYOTA'S COMMUNITY INVOLVEMENT ACTIVITIES

Toyota's domestic community involvement activities center around three main pillars. First is the promotion of science and technology, an area in which Toyota has been active since its establishment. Given the nature of Toyota's business, this is an area in which the company is expected to

---

6. The department's annual budget is set at around 2.5 percent of ordinary profits, which is relatively high compared to Toyota's peer companies.

play a role. A second priority set in April 1998 is support for global environment conservation. In 1997, Toyota launched an "Eco Project" to place greater emphasis on concern for the environment both in its normal line of business and in its philanthropic activities. The third priority is support for the arts and culture, or what the company terms "Mécénat activities."[7] Toyota believes that the enjoyment of the arts and culture is at the heart of all human interaction, thus emphasizing this area in particular.

Toyota's Mécénat activities are aimed at strengthening the cultural foundation of Japan's local communities by expanding the scope of cultural activities and educational opportunities, and by promoting and revitalizing local cultural activities. To achieve these goals, Toyota currently organizes five activity areas under the Mécénat umbrella; to each area the company gives full financial support as well as other forms of assistance, such as selling tickets and advertising events.

The first area is amateur classical music activities. For example, in collaboration with the Japan Amateur Orchestra League, Toyota co-hosts the Toyota Community Concert, the Toyota Youth Orchestra Camp, and the National Amateur Orchestra Festival. A second related area is activities of young artists, such as the Japan Young Artist Chamber Music Society, which was organized in 1991. The third area is arts and cultural activities by the disabled. In this field, Toyota has co-hosted the Toyota Able Art Forum since 1996 with the Association of Art, Culture, and People with Disabilities. This case will be discussed in more detail below. The fourth area is educating "liaison persons" for the arts. To this end, Toyota holds the Toyota Art Management Course, which seeks to train art managers who will be responsible for revitalizing the cultural activities of local communities. The final area is regional-level activities that are closely tied to the local community. The Toyota Community Art project, for example, exhibits artwork by young artists in the showrooms of local Toyota dealerships.

One theme common to all three pillars of domestic community involvement, and especially in the field of arts and culture, is Toyota's emphasis on revitalizing local communities in every part of Japan. Thus, it is imperative that Toyota work hand in hand with its car dealers across the country to effectively reach out to communities.[8]

7. *Mécénat* is the French term for patronage of the arts and culture.

8. Interview with Shuji Okabe, general manager of the Corporate Citizenship Department, Toyota Motor Corporation, at company headquarters in Tokyo, May 21, 1998.

TOYOTA'S PARTNERSHIPS WITH NGOS

In another effort to broaden the reach of its community involvement activities, Toyota actively collaborates with various NGOs in the areas of arts and culture and the environment. For example, in running the Toyota Art Management Course, the company works with the Association for Corporate Support of the Arts, which is a league of Japanese corporations focusing on corporate support for artistic and cultural activities.[9] In 1998, Toyota began various projects related to environmental education with the Japan Environmental Education Forum. Toyota and the Forum cooperate on a nature conservation project and are planning other projects as well.

Toyota considers NGOs to be the voice of society and views them as dedicated, active, and efficient. But sometimes that same dedication can make NGOs unbending and narrowly focused. Corporations tend to be rational since their ultimate goal is to maximize profits, but they are constrained by their responsibility to shareholders. Partnerships between these two types of organizations to address a shared agenda can produce a synergy that produces better results than either could achieve on its own.

Shuji Okabe, general manager of the Corporate Citizenship Department of Toyota Motor Corporation, described the general merits of corporate-NGO partnerships. From NGOs' point of view, such partnerships allow them to take advantage of the corporation's strengths, such as financial resources, human resources, space, and business know-how. In addition, working with corporations provides NGOs with the opportunity to enhance the quality and quantity of their activities and to expand their networks through meeting other NGOs in different fields or other corporations working in the same area.

The corporations, for their part, can tap the specialized information, networks, and human resources of the NGOs. Internally, working with NGOs can allow a corporation to create a new corporate culture by bringing in a variety of new values; externally, such partnerships enable the company to establish a new image for its community involvement activities. The NGOs can also act as the social conscience for the company.

Okabe stressed the important role of intermediary organizations in the

9. Support by the business community for projects not related to arts or culture is handled by the Committee on Corporate Philanthropy of Keidanren (Japan Federation of Economic Organizations).

partnership process and noted that Toyota prefers to form partnerships with NGOs that are active on a national scale and that also function as intermediaries, rather than working directly with individual, local NGOs. This is important in order for Toyota to appear fair, transparent, and neutral in its community activities.[10]

TOYOTA ABLE ART FORUM

The term "Able Art" was created in 1995 by Yasuo Harima, president of Tampopo no Ye, and his staff. Tampopo no Ye, or the House of Dandelions, is an NGO based in Nara Prefecture that has been assisting and supporting the artistic activities of people with disabilities for 30 years. In the United States and Europe, artistic activities and artwork by people with disabilities are often termed "Outsider Art." To emphasize more the enormous opportunities for and abilities of the disabled, Harima and his staff preferred the term "Able Art," which is meant to encompass not only people with disabilities but also the society that hosts and enables such activities and the citizens who appreciate the artwork.

The Able Art Movement began in 1995 with an Able Art Festival, which opened in Osaka in October 1995. The festival drew a great deal of attention and was well received by the media and the festival goers. The festival also captured the interest of a number of corporations, some of which were involved from the initial planning phase and others of which were motivated by the festival to become involved in the Able Art Movement.

THE PARTNERSHIP BUILDING PROCESS

Toyota's exposure to art by people with disabilities dates back to the early 1990s, when Toyota Foundation was supporting an institution for the disabled in Kyoto called the Mizunoki-Ryo (Dogwood Dormitory), which was active in encouraging artistic endeavors by the disabled. The members of Mizunoki-Ryo began to produce some excellent artwork that they wanted to share with the general public. Having visited the Mizunoki-Ryo and seen the artwork himself, Okabe was deeply impressed by the quality of the pieces and decided to sponsor an exhibition, which was organized by Mizunoki-Ryo and held in Yokohama in early 1995. Around the same time, Harima's Able Art Movement had also begun

10. Interview with Okabe.

to take shape, and the first Able Art Festival—a larger exhibit than the Yokohama show—was held in late 1995, with Toyota as one of the many sponsors.

Seeing the success of the Able Art Festival, and having been enlightened by the Able Art Movement, Toyota began to express interest in holding its own forums to bring the Movement to various parts of Japan. The company hoped not only to show the artwork but also to educate people about Able Art. At the same time, Harima was talking about the need for greater exposure for and public education about Able Art. Having worked together once on the Able Art Festival, Harima and Okabe decided to join forces again to organize the Toyota Able Art Forum, now the largest of the many Able Art Movement activities.

The Forum aims to foster an environment where artistic activities and artwork by people with disabilities are appreciated and socially recognized as art, rather than thought of just as an extension of rehabilitation efforts. Another important objective is to train people in local communities who can work toward creating such an environment.

The Forum is a project co-hosted and co-organized by Toyota Motor Corporation and the Association of Arts, Culture, and People with Disabilities, an NGO that was established in 1994 to expand the network of people involved in the dissemination of information available on the artistic and cultural activities of people with disabilities. The original plan to establish the Association came from Tampopo no Ye and its supporters. A need was felt to establish a new organization that would bridge various related activities throughout Japan and that could serve as an intermediary between people, organizations, and corporations. The Association began with Harima as one of the managing directors and a staff of two people seconded from Tampopo no Ye. The Association is an independent organization, but it works in close collaboration with Tampopo no Ye, which provides financial support.

Because the Association is an intermediary organization that operates nationwide, it met Toyota's criteria for NGO partners. In the case of Toyota Able Art Forum, the Association enables Toyota to work with NGOs like Tampopo no Ye and local communities.

SYMPOSIUMS AND WORKSHOPS OF TOYOTA ABLE ART FORUM

The Forum consists of two components: symposiums and workshops. The symposiums are held to educate citizens about Able Art and what it is trying to achieve. The workshops are aimed at training people to further promote artistic activities of people with disabilities. Typically, the work-shops are held in locations that have previously hosted a symposium.

The first symposium took place in Tokyo in March 1996 and was at-tended by close to 200 participants. The content of the meeting earned high praise, and buoyed by that success Toyota and the Association went on to hold five symposiums in fiscal 1996 (April 1996–March 1997). Seven new cities were added the following year, and each year the organizers returned to three of the previous year's symposium sites to hold more specialized workshops. To mark the success of the Forum, the partners also convened a special forum in Tokyo in 1999, drawing on experiences and feed-back from past symposiums and workshops.

THE ROLES OF THE PARTNERS

The responsibility for managing and running the Toyota Able Art Forum series is divided among the various actors involved in the project. The major task of Toyota Motor Corporation is to provide financial resources, without which this project would cease to exist. Toyota is also in charge of the overall planning of the Forum, as well as of determining the future direction of the project. The planning of the location, dates, and frame-work of symposiums and workshops is a joint effort between Toyota and the Association, although Toyota has final say. The company also provides other support such as staff, technology, know-how, and its network of people and information. For example, Toyota does all of the printing of the brochures, papers, and pamphlets for the Able Art Forum in-house.

Since Toyota's knowledge of art in general—and particularly of art by people with disabilities—is limited, the Association is responsible for the content of the symposiums and workshops. Each year, the staff of the Association submits to Toyota a preliminary agenda along with an annual budget. Toyota then incorporates its own priorities and schedule into the plan, and the two sides come up with a final plan. The Association re-ceives 10 percent of the total annual project budget as overhead from To-yota. Although the Association's staff is small, roughly one-third of their time is spent traveling across Japan to oversee the preparations of the Fo-rum, and they are in daily contact with their counterparts at Toyota.

Once the content of the symposiums and workshops is decided, the Association then decides on the locations for holding the Forum. The cities are selected by the Association and Tampopo no Ye on the basis of future potential for becoming a host community for art by people with disabilities. The Association is also responsible for recruiting panelists and organizing the exhibits. In line with the mission to localize each of the Forums, the themes and the panelists are chosen so that special features of the particular city or region are reflected in the discussions.

Toyota tries to involve its dealers from the selected communities in the partnership, and lists the names of the dealers as co-organizers. However, because Toyota and the dealer companies are separate entities, the extent of Toyota Motor Corporation's control is limited to asking the local dealers to distribute the pamphlets and to publicize the symposiums and workshops to the local media. The degree of the local dealers' involvement varies depending on their interests and commitments.

EXECUTIVE COMMITTEES

The symposiums and workshops are run by executive committees that are established in the local communities and that draw on the participation of local NGOs, citizens, and occasionally government officials. Thus, the Toyota Able Art Forum not only is a partnership between the corporation and the NGO but also involves a much broader spectrum of actors. This decentralized approach to running the events is a unique feature of the Forum that fosters artistic and cultural activities which are truly rooted in the local communities.

Each committee oversees the preparations for the symposium or workshop to be held in its community. One key person from the local community—found through the network of Tampopo no Ye—is assigned to assume the central role in organizing the committee; that person chooses the rest of the committee members. An ideal executive committee would include members from the local government, local NGOs and welfare institutions, as well as scholars and artists. The committees serve as a forum for various actors in the local community to interact by working together for a common goal. This experience not only benefits the forum but also enhances local-level community activities in general.

ACHIEVEMENTS OF THE PARTNERSHIP

MEETING THE GOALS OF THE PROJECT

Both Toyota and the Association have been pleased with the outcome of the project to date. One example of a particularly successful Toyota Able Art Forum is the experience of Kanazawa City, where the project served as a catalyst in promoting local-level activities. A symposium was first held there in 1997, followed by a workshop the next year. One participant in the symposium was the director of the Kanazawa Citizens and Art Center, a 24-hour public art facility built by the city. Deeply impressed by the Forum, he volunteered to organize the executive committee the following year. He subsequently organized an Able Art Exhibition at his Art Center, for which the financial support was provided by a local sake brewer who had also attended the symposium.

In addition to strengthening the Able Art Movement, this example epitomizes Toyota's goal of promoting community activities organized by local people for local citizens. It touched both the local government, as represented by the Art Center, and local businesses, as represented by the sake brewer. The success of Kanazawa City has given the organizers confidence to further expand the Toyota Able Art Forum throughout Japan.

MEETING THE GOALS OF THE PARTNERSHIP

According to both organizations, the four-year partnership between Toyota and the Association of Art, Culture, and People with Disabilities has provided a valuable experience for both the corporation and the NGO. Through their combined efforts and resources, they have been able to conduct a unique event that neither organization would have been able to accomplish on its own.

Toyota has been able to add a new dimension to its philanthropic efforts and to expand the scope of its community involvement activities through the support of artistic activities by people with disabilities. By working closely with NGOs and with the various local communities, this project has also enhanced the corporate image of Toyota. While Okabe did mention in his interview that "the NGOs gain more from the corporate-NGO partnership than the corporation,"[11] his comments to an advertisement industry magazine shed light on how Toyota views the potential benefits of corporate-NGO partnership. In talking about the ultimate motive of profit maximization, Okabe stated, "Collaborating with NPOs [nonprofit organizations] and having employee volunteers . . . is very effective in creating an image of a company that is into community involvement, and also in creating an image that the corporate culture is always evolving. In the long run, these activities are very effective in establishing a unique corporate image."[12]

11. Ibid.

12. *Senden Kaigi* [Advertisement Conference] (March 1998), p. 26–27.

Okabe also noted that although Toyota is happy with the partnership and with the success of the project, the partnership could probably be improved significantly if the partner NGO was at a more advanced stage of development. As is the case with many Japanese NGOs, the Association suffers from a lack of staff, capital, and professional experience that impedes its operations.

The Association, for its part, has benefited from Toyota's financial and nonfinancial contributions. The Toyota Able Art Forum project has offered the Association an arena in which to promote the Able Art Movement and to expand its function as an intermediary organization. Toyota's support has also included an institution-building element, since Toyota is the only corporation that gives financial support to the Association itself.[13]

Yoshiyasu Ota, a staff member of the Association, noted that the one potential drawback to working with Toyota is the exclusivity of the partnership, which may pose a constraint on the Able Art Movement. This can also be said of similar Able Art projects with other corporations. The Able Art Movement consists of many activities conducted in partnership with corporations. For example, a major construction company, Taisei, provided support to organize an art exhibition at the Tokyo Metropolitan Museum of Art in 1997. Another major partner corporation is Fuji Xerox Co. Ltd., which has been co-hosting a separate "Able Art Workshop" with the Association since 1997. While these and other partnerships between the Association and various corporations are a sign of the successful growth of interest in the Able Art Movement, coordination among the corporations seems to be lacking.

Because of the success of the Toyota Able Art Forum, it should be interesting to watch what Toyota does next. As Toyota has always been one step ahead of other corporations in corporate community involvement activities, the company may enter another stage of corporate philanthropy in the coming years. For the time being, however, the company seems to be content to continue the Forum, and the next big partnership project is not in sight.

Okabe noted that Toyota is still faced with the major challenge of evaluating and measuring the success of the Forum objectively in terms of whether the project is meeting the needs of society and individuals.

13. Of the Association's ¥55 million operating fund, ¥10 million comes from Toyota, ¥20 million from the Tokyo Metropolitan Museum of Art, and ¥2 million from members.

Without guidance of this kind, Okabe noted, Toyota is unable to move ahead, let alone formulate a mid-term to long-term strategy. For the immediate future, however, Toyota still sees areas that need to be tapped for the Toyota Able Art Forum, such as the large Kanto region around Tokyo, and it is planning to expand the number of symposiums and workshops to be held in 1999 and 2000.

10 Yasuda Kasai and the Japan Environmental Education Forum

Mio Kawashima

UNTIL quite recently, Japan's second largest non-life insurance company, Yasuda Fire and Marine Insurance Co., Ltd. (Yasuda Kasai) was perhaps best known to the Japanese public for its taste in artwork. The establishment of the Seiji Togo Memorial Yasuda Kasai Museum of Art in 1976 and the purchase of Vincent van Gogh's "Sunflowers" for the museum in 1987 had earned Yasuda Kasai a reputation as a patron of the arts. A decade later, however, Yasuda Kasai has created a new image for itself—that of an environmentally conscious, "green" company concerned about the community.

How did a traditional Japanese financial institution come to be active in environmental issues and community activities in such a short period of time? The answer lies in personal initiative, strong leadership, and a systematic, companywide approach to the environment. Under the guidance of its chairman and chief executive officer, Yasuo Goto, Yasuda Kasai decided to combine its objectives as a profit-oriented business with its motivation as an environmentally oriented corporate citizen to create a new corporate philosophy: Yasuda Kasai would strive to become "a company that is kind to people and nature."[1] In keeping with this philosophy, the company teamed up with a nonprofit organization, the Japan Environmental Education Forum (JEEF), to conduct an educational initiative for

1. As of April 1, 1999, Mr. Goto became Corporate Counsellor and Director Chairman Emeritus of Yasuda Kasai.

the public on environmental issues. By bringing to bear the complementary resources of both organizations, this partnership has benefited all parties involved and it has successfully reached its objective of educating the public.

YASUDA KASAI

The story of Yasuda Kasai begins at its establishment in 1888 as the first company in Japan providing insurance protection against fires. Over the past century, the company has developed diverse business operations in non-life insurance and other financial services. As of March 1998, Yasuda Kasai employed nearly 12,000 people, with 517 offices and 74,600 agents throughout Japan, and 37 overseas representative offices.

CORPORATE PHILANTHROPY: FROM ART TO ENVIRONMENT

Yasuda Kasai has been a keen patron of the arts since the early 1920s, supporting numerous artists over the years. In 1976, the Yasuda Kasai Art Foundation was established to promote the arts in Japan and overseas. The Foundation was also responsible for managing a new art gallery, the Seiji Togo Memorial Yasuda Kasai Museum of Art, the opening of which was planned to coincide with the completion of the company's new headquarters in the Shinjuku district of Tokyo. "Sunflowers" was purchased for the gallery to commemorate the 100th anniversary of the company, and also to boost the number of visitors to the gallery. Although criticized by many at the time as the epitome of the extravagance that was so prevalent during the "bubble" economy—Yasuda Kasai paid an unprecedented US$39.9 million for the painting—Goto and those close to the company stress the positive impact the painting has had on Yasuda Kasai's insurance business. They point to the increased visibility of the company and the subsequent business connections that the purchase generated, referring to this as the "Sunflower Effect."

In addition to the arts, Yasuda provides funding for charitable organizations and for research on social welfare issues through the Yasuda Kasai Foundation, which was established in 1977. Additional philanthropic activities include the promotion of sporting events in local communities, such as the nationwide Masters Table Tennis Tournament for adults and senior citizens.

In the 1990s, the focus of Yasuda's support expanded to include environmental issues. The initiative for this change came primarily from

Goto, who was deeply concerned with the impact of the ongoing degradation of the global environment both on people and on the future economic activity of corporations. The insurance sector is particularly
susceptible to payment claims resulting from natural disasters, many of
which are now being linked to the depletion of, or disregard for, natural
resources by humans. Despite his personal convictions, however, Goto
had not translated his beliefs into substantial efforts by the company. As
he admitted in a newspaper interview, in the past he "thought the firm
was making a significant enough social contribution by running an art
museum."[2]

The turning point in his thinking came in 1992, when Richard Wein-
stein, chairman of The Nature Conservancy (TNC), a well-established
nongovernmental organization (NGO) based in Washington, D.C., approached Yasuda Kasai to ask for its support of a TNC project in Indonesia. At the time, TNC was actively seeking to expand its financial base
for its Asia program. Yasuda was initially reluctant to extend its philanthropy into a completely new area, given that it already had established
itself as a supporter of the arts. Goto, however, instinctively sensed the
value of this project and, given his personal concern for the environment,
decided to proceed.[3]

This project introduced Goto to various environmental issues, including nature conservation, and the experience peaked his interest. He was
also impressed by the professionalism and expertise of TNC, realizing
for the first time that such NGOs exist. As a result, Goto expressed interest in attending the Earth Summit in Rio de Janeiro in 1992. Keidanren
(Japan Federation of Economic Organizations), which was having difficulty recruiting high-ranking corporate representatives to attend, asked
Goto to go not just as a participant but as the head of the Keidanren delegation to the summit.

This event proved to be a watershed for Goto personally and for Yasuda Kasai. Since that time, Goto has gained a great deal of knowledge
about the field and has become a leading figure in advocating corporate
responses to environmental issues. Goto also took on the chairmanship of
the Keidanren Nature Conservation Fund, which supports the conservation

2. "Environmental Dues Seen as Cost for Firms That Deserve to Thrive," *Japan Times*,
September 13, 1996.

3. The donation was ultimately channeled through the Keidanren Nature Conservation
Fund rather than being made directly to TNC in order to support the new Keidanren
mechanism.

activities of NGOs in developing nations. At the same time, he began to infuse Yasuda Kasai's own philanthropic activities with a new focus on environmental issues.

COMMUNITY INVOLVEMENT AS BUSINESS STRATEGY

In 1988, Yasuda Kasai added a dimension of social responsibility to its corporate strategy when it announced that the company's new objective was "to incorporate achievement with virtue as a principle of business." "Virtue" was intended to signify the attitude and behavior of the company and its employees toward society. In addition to being virtuous, however, philanthropy and community involvement also make good business sense. Insurance is a person-to-person business, and people buy insurance based on their trust of the salespeople. For that reason, strong links with the local community can have a positive impact on the company's sales. Yasuda Kasai employees across Japan are urged to actively participate in local community events and activities, and the local branch managers are encouraged to become members of NGOs in their area. The host communities naturally welcome such gestures, and many local sales agencies have expressed their wish to become a Yasuda Kasai agency because the company is seen as being community-friendly.

Concern for the environment was also seen by Yasuda Kasai as a way to give back to the community. As Goto stated, "Our company exists with our customers. The number of customers will increase if we do things that will make [them] happy. This is the way for a corporation to flourish. Valuing the global environment is the way for corporations to flourish in the coming age."[4]

YASUDA KASAI'S EFFORTS
TO ADDRESS ENVIRONMENTAL ISSUES

The earliest efforts by Yasuda Kasai to address environmental issues date back to 1989, when Goto assigned Hissho Kitamura, who was then the director of the President's Office, to be in charge of global environmental issues. Initially, Kitamura alone handled this task. He had no staff, and there were no specific projects for him to carry out. His activities were therefore limited to suggesting ways for the company to conserve

---

4. "Environmental Issues and Corporations No. 4—A Corporation That Is Kind to Both Humans and Nature," by Shigeyuki Okajima, *Yomiuri AD Report OJO* (July 1998), p. 20.

natural resources, such as recycling paper and eliminating disposable chopsticks from the cafeteria. In 1990, Yasuda Kasai also established a Global Environment Risk Management Office as part of the Department of Technology Services. That office's activities included seminars on environmental law and the publishing of newsletters.

It was not until 1991, however, that the company adopted a more systematic approach. That year, an internal committee was established called the ECO Committee, which sought to promote more wide-ranging environmental activities and to examine ways in which Yasuda Kasai as a company could address environmental issues. Manager-level employees participated in three subcommittees of the ECO Committee that focused on conservation of energy, community involvement, and non-life insurance related goods and services. The subcommittee on energy conservation introduced an environment management system within the company to conserve energy and resources. The subcommittee on community involvement looked at how Yasuda Kasai could contribute to society. The subcommittee on product development looked at ways in which the company could incorporate efforts toward the environment into its main insurance business line, and eventually introduced new products such as Environment Impairment Liability Insurance and the Environment Conservation Support Credit Card. ECO committees were also set up in offices across Japan to plan and promote projects at the local level.

COMMUNITY INVOLVEMENT ACTIVITIES

Yasuda Kasai's community involvement activities incorporate both company efforts and individual involvement by employees. At the corporate level, Yasuda places emphasis on environmental education that promotes awareness among the general public. Accordingly, Yasuda runs a series of lectures, the Environmental Public Course for Citizens, in collaboration with JEEF, as will be described in greater detail below.

Yasuda also believes that it is important to encourage its employees to volunteer for environmental conservation activities, which not only benefit the environment but also provide a learning opportunity for the employees. After some debate within the ECO Committee over the appropriate role of the company in promoting employee volunteerism, the Chikyu (Earth) Club was formed in 1993 as a voluntary organization within the company, and from 1998 all Yasuda employees became members. The club has branches in Yasuda's regional offices, and its activities are organized and managed by some 300 "key persons"—volunteers from Yasuda offices across Japan who match employee volunteers with projects such as beach clean-up campaigns and charity bazaars. In addition, the company will soon be offering an in-house computer network to provide employees with information on different community involvement activities in which they can participate.

Another method of encouraging volunteerism emerged in 1993, when Yasuda began a leave-of-absence program for those volunteering to work with nonprofit organizations. Employees are entitled to apply for paid "volunteer leave" of up to three years, and a "volunteer holiday" (also paid) of up to 20 days. Thus the company is attempting to be a catalyst for promoting employee participation.

FURTHER DEVELOPMENTS IN SYSTEMATIZING YASUDA'S ENVIRONMENTAL EFFORTS

In 1992, based on the recommendation of the ECO Committee, the Department of Global Environment was established, and this department became the Secretariat for the ECO Committee. Kitamura became the first general manager of the department, overseeing a staff of eight employees. Currently, the Department of Global Environment coordinates all of Yasuda's environment-related projects.

In addition to these structural changes, Yasuda Kasai established a "Fundamental Policy on Environmental Issues" in 1994; this policy was adopted as the Yasuda Fire and Marine Global Environment Charter in July 1998. With regard to community involvement, the Charter states that "Yasuda, as a company aiming to care for people and nature, will actively support social contribution activities and environmental education. Further, Yasuda promotes and strongly supports voluntary efforts of individual employees as 'global citizens' and 'righteous members of family and society' in environmental conservation and social contributions."[5]

In 1999, Yasuda established the Global Environmental Foundation as part of the Department of Global Environment, and the Foundation is now co-host of the Public Course. The Foundation will focus on human resource development for professionals in the field of the environment and will grant scholarships and awards to those in Japan and Asia.

5. Yasuda Kasai Web site < http://www/yasuda.co.jp > (November 1998).

PARTNERSHIP WITH JEEF

RATIONALE FOR CORPORATE-NGO PARTNERSHIP

Solving global environmental issues will require full participation of all members of society, and Goto has become increasingly convinced of the complementary roles that the various sectors can play. While private companies are constrained by their obligation to earn profits, civil society organizations are subject to no such limitations. This "enables them to quickly detect changes and issues in society, and then undertake swift, flexible, and well-adapted action."[6] In fact, Goto feels that the business world can learn a great deal from the passion and sense of mission demonstrated by NGOs, as well as their ability to act decisively to fulfill that mission.[7]

Yasuda Kasai's corporate philosophy also reflects the belief that NGOs will play a more prominent role in Japanese society in the future. The Law to Promote Specified Nonprofit Activities, which was the product of the joint efforts of politicians, the business sector, and the nonprofit sector, was enacted on December 1, 1998, and is expected to strengthen the institutional base of NGOs and allow them to expand the scope of their activities. Goto, however, is fully aware of the limitations of Japanese NGOs as compared to their counterparts in other countries—especially those addressing environmental issues. Despite the improved legal framework, Japanese NGOs still lack a strong institutional base and professional staff, which makes it difficult to raise funds to carry out their mission. As Goto has noted, "Most Japanese NPOs [nonprofit organizations] do not have the experience or achievements to convince companies [to support them]."[8] In this respect, the corporate sector can help strengthen NGOs by providing financial support and human resources. In return, corporations can gain access to the knowledge base and network of the NGOs in the field. An additional incentive, of course, is the marketing advantage generated by the public perception of a corporation working closely with an NGO for the good of society.

6. "An Overview of Civil Society," a speech given by Yasuo Goto for the U.S.-Japan Common Agenda in a Global Context, Civil Society Workshop, February 2–3, 1998, Washington, D.C.

7. Ibid.

8. "Environmental Dues Seen as Cost for Firms That Deserve to Thrive," *Japan Times*, September 13, 1996.

Yasuda Kasai's main community involvement project, the Environ-mental Public Course for Citizens, exemplifies this type of synergistic relationship. Beginning in 1993, the program has been conducted in part-nership with JEEF. As a result, Yasuda Kasai has been able to expand its knowledge of the field and its human network, thereby enhancing its ability to engage in environment-related activities. JEEF, for its part, has been able to acquire the financial and technical support needed to run the program effectively.

PARTNERSHIP BUILDING PROCESS

In 1991, when the ECO Committee's Community Involvement Subcom-mittee was considering how Yasuda Kasai could address environmental issues, there was a great deal of debate regarding how to proceed. It was initially agreed that the company would make a large donation to an NGO working in the field of environmental education, an area that Yasuda Ka-sai designated a priority. Since many NGOs had already approached the company for support, the subcommittee decided that it would pick an appropriate NGO from among them and make the donation.

During the same period that those deliberations were going on, how-ever, Yasuda representatives happened to attend a Keidanren seminar on "Corporations and the Environment," in which Shigeyuki Okajima, man-aging director of JEEF and deputy editor of the *Yomiuri Shimbun* news-paper, was also a participant. During the seminar, Okajima raised the issue of the lack of opportunities for the Japanese public to learn about the environment. As one idea for addressing this problem, he asked if corporations would be willing to lend floor space in their office buildings to hold lectures on the environment.

Around this same time, one of Yasuda's competitors made a large finan-cial donation to Keio University to create an environmental lecture series with the name of the company attached to the course. Yasuda Kasai real-ized that merely donating funds to an environmental NGO would not be considered innovative, nor would it effectively demonstrate the company's commitment to environmental issues and to the community. Instead, the company could have a greater impact by involving itself in the implemen-tation and management of a project initiated jointly with an NGO. Yasuda Kasai decided to accept Okajima's proposal to co-host the environmental lecture series, using the main auditorium at the company's headquarters.

JEEF originated in a 1987 gathering of individuals to develop appro-priate environmental education programs for schoolchildren, youth, adults, and corporations. In 1992, those individuals formed a voluntary organization, which was then incorporated in 1997 under the authority of the Environment Agency. JEEF's core missions are to create nature schools across Japan, to promote environmental education for the corporate sector and the general public, and to support environmental education in developing nations.

Acording to Okajima, JEEF was initially happy just to have the space to hold the seminars. Conducting environmental education inside a corporation's building allows the seminar to be incorporated into the company's corporate philanthropy in a more meaningful way. However, Yasuda wanted to play a more active role in the project, and thus the partnership began.

A preparatory committee was formed consisting of staff from JEEF and Yasuda's Department of Global Environment, and the details of the program quickly took shape. The Environmental Public Course for Citizens was planned as a university-course-equivalent lecture series on environmental issues, the main objective of which was to raise awareness and understanding of environmental issues among the general public. The course offers an integrated approach, covering political, economic, and business perspectives, as well as educational and consumer issues. In the first half of each year, an "Introduction to the Environment" series is offered, comprised of ten bimonthly lectures. The program for the second half of the year consists of two special series of four to five lectures, each addressing more specific topics such as waste management, global warming, or CO_2 emissions.

JEEF is responsible for organizing the content of the lecture series and deciding on the topics and speakers. Its strong network of experts in the field has allowed it to draw on prestigious resource persons as speakers. In addition to providing financial resources and a venue for the lectures, Yasuda Kasai has also invested some ¥100 million (US$864,000 at ¥115.70 = US$1) for state-of-the-art audio-visual equipment for the auditorium. Yasuda employees participate by setting up the auditorium, preparing hand-outs, communicating with the invited lecturers, sending out invitations to prospective participants, and handling advertising and publicity.

RESULTS OF THE PARTNERSHIP

Since the first lecture in October 1993, more than 3,500 individuals have participated in the course, and it continues to attract interest. About half of those attending are from corporations, many of whom have just been assigned to the environment departments in their own companies. Because the Public Course provides such thorough coverage of the topic, it has become famous as a training course for corporate staff. Other participants include NGO staff, public servants, university students, housewives, teachers, and professors.

The success of the program has affected Yasuda Kasai in a number of ways. The program has earned the Department for Global Environment higher status within the company, and employee morale has been boosted by the company's improved public image and by the opportunity to work with an NGO—a phenomenon that is relatively new in Japan and certainly new to Yasuda Kasai. Externally, the NGO partnership and environmental activities have contributed to Yasuda's business operations by allowing the company to differentiate itself from its competitors—an important factor given the greater competition it faces in the current sluggish economy. This is not to say, however, that the company's efforts to address environmental issues were motivated by profits. It was precisely because the initial motivation was one of genuine concern for the environment that it has been able to succeed.

The company has also become more understanding of NGOs, their activities, and their mission through working with JEEF, and this has prompted Yasuda Kasai to begin seconding its staff to NGOs. Yasuda staff worked with The Nature Conservancy in 1993 and 1994, and with the Wild Bird Society of Japan in 1995 and 1996.

REASONS FOR SUCCESS

Both Yasuda Kasai and JEEF have been pleased with the results of their partnership. The course has provided high-quality lectures and has been well attended, prompting Yasuda Kasai to extend its support for the course indefinitely. By working together, both organizations have been able to produce results that they could not have achieved on their own.

Two primary factors have contributed to the success of the program. The first is the strength of the NGO partner. The quality of the Environmental Public Course for Citizens, and the subsequent popularity of the course, is owed entirely to JEEF. The NGO's active participation and large network have enabled organization of a highly intellectual and professional team of resource persons.

The second factor is a well-balanced partnership based on mutual trust between JEEF and the Department of Global Environment at Yasuda. Mutual respect existed from the very beginning between the two organizations. According to Okajima, many companies tend to behave arrogantly toward NGOs. Fortunately, Yasuda Kasai did not behave that way; on the contrary, it was eager to learn from JEEF's expertise. Yasuda's attitude may have been influenced by the fact that the three representatives of JEEF who came to talk to the company during initial meetings were not full-time NGO staff, but rather a journalist, a bureaucrat from the Environment Agency, and a scholar. Having the full backing of Goto from the beginning also reinforced the partnership.

CHALLENGES AHEAD

It is evident from the experience of Yasuda Kasai that the presence of a strong personal and corporate commitment to environmental issues is critical to success, as is the presence of strong leadership. Over the past decade, Goto has become a key figure not only in Yasuda's activities but also in the activities of Japan's corporate sector as a whole. In 1998, his efforts earned him a place on the United Nations Environment Program Global 500 Roll of Honor. Most important, he has passed his enthusiasm and commitment on to the Department of Global Environment and to all of the employees at Yasuda Kasai. This strong leadership has allowed the company, in a relatively short period of time, to establish a reputation not only for being committed to environmental issues but also for being supportive of civil society organizations.

Now that Yasuda Kasai has the organizational capacity, skill, structure, network, and reputation to carry out community activities on environmental issues, the next challenge for the company is deciding where to go from here. With the present activities being so successful and well received, there is little room to reverse course, but given the state of the Japanese economy, one cannot predict the future with confidence. Maintaining the current level of morale and commitment of both the company and the employees is a critical issue, especially when top management is bound to change at some point in the future. One way in which the company has sought to ensure continuity was to change its corporate philosophy to include the aim of being "a company that is kind to people and nature." According to Takashi Seo, deputy general manager of the Global Environment Department, the task of incorporating that strategy into the company's daily operations and actions is a major challenge facing his department, and project teams have been organized to examine the issue.

How the company will perceive working with NGOs is another issue. When asked whether Yasuda Kasai wanted to form other partnerships with NGOs, Kitamura replied that there are no such plans for the fore-seeable future. Whether this is because Yasuda places great importance and emphasis on the current partnership it has with JEEF, or because Ya-suda perceives its current efforts to be enough, is unclear.

Goto has said that, "If a company wasn't making profits, it wouldn't be alive. If a company ignores the global environment, it wouldn't de-serve to be alive."[9] It is very much hoped that this sentiment will remain with the company, and that the company's success in working with JEEF will become a stepping stone for further activities in the community.

9. Ibid.

11 Keidanren Nature Conservation Fund

Mio Kawashima

THE environmental movement in Japan has for decades been a battle waged between environmentalists and corporations. The primary objective of most Japanese environmental nongovernmental organizations (NGOs) has been to combat industrial pollution—a byproduct of the high-growth policies of post–World War II Japan—and thus they have traditionally been critical of and confrontational toward corporations, which they viewed as the source of deadly chemical waste and toxins. The corporations have stood on the other side of the battlefield, denying culpability. They were represented by Keidanren (Japan Federation of Economic Organizations), the influential federation of Japan's leading businesses, which joined its members in claiming that companies were not responsible for pollution. In the 1970s, the government finally began to take action to address the problem of industrial pollution, and the business community reluctantly followed suit. Despite substantial progress in taming industrial pollution however, the business community and citizen groups remained hostile toward each other into the 1990s.

Given that climate, it came as a surprise to many when Keidanren announced the adoption of a Global Environmental Charter in April 1991. Not only did the charter acknowledge corporate responsibility for environmental degradation, but it also set environmental standards for Japanese corporate activities both in Japan and abroad. The charter was translated into action in 1992, when the Keidanren Nature Conservation Fund (KNCF) was established to engage Keidanren member companies in nature conservation projects. KNCF serves as an intermediary organization, encouraging and facilitating corporate support for NGOs, and thereby building trust and cooperation where there once was only animosity. As a result, many of those same corporations that were once reviled by environmental NGOs are now working with them through KNCF to protect endangered species, reforest regions throughout Asia, and promote ecotourism and sustainable agriculture.

KEIDANREN

Keidanren was established shortly after the end of World War II to help Japan recover from the devastation of the war. It is a private, nonprofit economic organization representing trade associations and major corporations. As of July 1998, Keidanren's membership roster included 121 trade associations and 1,011 corporations. The organization's stated objective is "to work for a resolution of the major problems facing the business community in Japan and abroad, and to contribute to sound development of the Japanese and world economies."[1] To achieve this goal, Keidanren creates committees to ascertain the opinions of the business community on specific issues, and then conveys those opinions to the government and political parties. Another function of Keidanren is to promote better corporate citizenship by setting guidelines for its corporate members on ethical behavior and on environmentally sound practices. In this and other ways, Keidanren works to strengthen the ties between the corporate sector and consumers, labor organizations, nonprofit organizations, and other sectors of society.

PHILANTHROPIC ACTIVITIES OF KEIDANREN

For many years, Keidanren has coordinated fund raising for various causes, both domestic and international, by utilizing what has become known as the "Keidanren Method." Through this method, domestic and overseas nonprofit organizations seeking financial support from the Japanese business sector bring their proposals to Keidanren, which first assesses whether a proposal meets its fund-raising guidelines. If it does, then a target fund-raising figure is agreed upon, and a certain percentage of that figure is allotted to member industrial associations and corporations as their suggested contribution. The nonprofit organization then

---

1. Keidanren Web site < http://www.keidanren.or.jp > (November 1998).

approaches those associations and corporations to request the specified amount. In the past, although the process was voluntary, Keidanren's suggestions had significant influence with its members. More recently, that influence has waned somewhat, as corporations are increasingly pursuing their respective philanthropic interests. One advantage of the Keidanren Method has been that individual companies need not examine the project proposals themselves. The method also enables them to consult with peers in the business world regarding the final amount of their donations. Fifty to 100 projects receive funding each year under the Keidanren Method, and the total amount of donations ranges from ¥5 billion to ¥10 billion (US$43.2 million to US$86.4 million at ¥115.70 = US$1).[2]

Although the Keidanren Method served its purpose, the organization became conscious of the need to improve its philanthropic activities in the late 1980s, as many Japanese companies started setting up factories in the United States. From 1985 to 1990, the number of factories in the United States owned by Japanese corporations jumped from 250 to 1,600. The increase in foreign direct investment was partly a response to the much criticized trade surplus between the United States and Japan, but it was also fueled by the appreciation of the yen following the 1985 Plaza Accord. These Japanese corporations operating in local American communities quickly learned the importance of becoming "good corporate citizens" through philanthropic and community involvement activities.

In response to this trend, Keidanren undertook a number of new initiatives. In cooperation with the Japan Center for International Exchange (JCIE), it dispatched in 1988 a study mission to the United States focusing on the theme of good corporate citizenship. The following year, Keidanren established the Council for Better Corporate Citizenship (CBCC) as an incorporated association that serves as an intermediary, allowing corporations to make tax-deductible donations to overseas organizations.[3] Also in 1989, JCIE and Keidanren held a seminar in Tokyo on the theme of "Becoming Good Corporate Citizens in American Communities: New Challenges for Japanese Corporations in an Interdependent World." Attending this seminar was the late Natsuaki Fusano, Keidanren's senior managing director at the time, who had led the study mission to

2. *White Paper on Corporate Philanthropy in Japan 1996* (Tokyo: Keidanren), 1996, p. 48.

3. Under current Japanese law, the deductibility of donations to charitable organizations within Japan is limited. Donations to overseas organizations can be deducted, but only when channeled through one of a handful of specified organizations.

the United States the previous year. Having been inspired by the "percent clubs" of the United States, whereby companies donate a certain percentage of their pretax profits to philanthropic activities, Fusano suggested that Keidanren establish a "1% Club." Keidanren's One Percent Club was officially inaugurated in 1990.[4] As of March 1999, membership, which is strictly voluntary, stood at 281 corporate members and 1,336 individual members.[5]

Also in 1990, Keidanren established the Committee on Corporate Philanthropy to promote greater rapport between the corporate sector and the community and to encourage corporations to fulfill their social responsibilities. Approximately 240 companies are currently members of this committee. These member corporations are represented by their philanthropy managers, who participate in various subcommittees that focus on specific issues, such as understanding the basic principles of community involvement or developing concrete ways to practice community involvement activities. One subcommittee, the Special Subcommittee on Philanthropy Infrastructure Logistics, was particularly active during the campaign to pass the Law to Promote Specified Nonprofit Activities (the NPO Law), which facilitates incorporation of nonprofit organizations in Japan.[6] In anticipation of greater opportunities for partnerships between corporations and NGOs, the subcommittee worked closely with NGO leaders lobbying for passage of the bill.

BACKGROUND TO THE ESTABLISHMENT
OF THE FUND

The Keidanren Nature Conservation Fund is an important component of Keidanren's philanthropic initiatives. Established in 1992, the year of the Earth Summit, the Fund provides financial assistance to environmental

4. Tadashi Yamamoto, "The Evolution of Japan's International Giving and Its Future Prospects," in *International Grantmaking* (New York: The Foundation Center), 1997, p. 125–126. See also *International Philanthropy Project of the Japan Center for International Exchange: A Case Study* (Tokyo: Japan Center for International Exchange), 1991.

5. Member companies are expected to donate at least 1 percent of their pretax profits under a voluntary agreement, and individual members are also expected to donate no less than 1 percent of their taxable income. Corporate donations usually exceed the 1 percent benchmark, normally fluctuating around 2.7 percent. Figures provided by Emiko Nagasawa, Business & Society Group, Social Affairs Bureau of Keidanren.

6. The NPO Law was promulgated in March 1998 and enacted in December 1998.

NGOs conducting nature conservation projects overseas. Its establishment was significant both because it symbolized the business community's acknowledgment of the importance of environmentalism and because it offered financial support to NGOs with which the business community had in the past often had a confrontational relationship. To understand just how large a step this was, it is helpful to briefly trace the path of the Japanese business community from the period of industrial pollution to the present.

INDUSTRIAL POLLUTION

Following the end of World War II, Japan set itself on a track of high economic growth. Speedy industrial development became the highest of economic and political priorities no matter what the cost—and often the cost turned out to be deadly. Serious, and sometimes fatal, illnesses caused by pollution were discovered in industrial areas during the 1950s. Perhaps the best known example was the infamous Minamata Disease, caused by consumption of fish contaminated by mercury discharged from chemical plants. Officially "discovered" in 1956, victims of this disease suffered from paralysis, deformity of limbs, and convulsions. Despite having known that factories were disposing of deadly chemical waste in the rivers and oceans, the Ministry of International Trade and Industry did nothing to address the problem until the end of the 1960s. In the meantime, additional cases of pollution-related epidemics were discovered, and by the 1970s the victims had begun taking legal action against corporations.

The first step toward correcting this problem came in 1970, when the so-called antipollution Diet was convened. That year, the Diet successfully passed a series of antipollution laws and moved to create the Environment Agency, which was established in 1971. One new law, the General Pollution Law, made it possible for the victims of pollution-induced illnesses to press criminal charges against corporations. These laws created a strong incentive for the business community to develop antipollution technology. Just as Japan was able to achieve economic growth in a short period of time, so too was it able to quickly adopt new antipollution, or "green," technologies and turn them into a new industry.

THE KEIDANREN GLOBAL ENVIRONMENTAL CHARTER

By the 1990s, Japan had industrial pollution largely under control, and there was talk of presenting Japan as a model case at the Earth Summit in 1992. Keidanren, seeing that business communities in other countries were starting to take responsibility for addressing environmental issues, had begun to examine what it could do. Around this same time, Gaishi Hiraiwa, chairman of TEPCO (Tokyo Electric Power Company Inc.), became the chairman of Keidanren and introduced his philosophy of "*kyosei*," or "symbiosis," stressing the importance of coexistence between corporations and community; between corporations and individuals; between corporations and the global community; and between corporations and the surrounding natural environment. Hiraiwa's experience at TEPCO had sensitized him to the importance of good corporate-community relations, and from that he was able to see the importance of a larger relationship between the corporate sector and the global environment.

In 1991, the International Chamber of Commerce, under the leadership of chief executive officers of big conglomerates such as Dupont, announced an Environmental Charter that was then adopted by many corporations. Keidanren proposed to use this as a model to create its own Environmental Charter, but its members reacted negatively to the idea. Many Japanese chief executive officers and Keidanren staff feared that the charter would bind corporate activities substantially, since it included clauses calling on corporations to give full consideration to the environment of all areas or regions in which they operate and to consider environmental concerns from the initial research and development stage of their operations.

Despite strong resistance, Hiraiwa held firmly to his convictions and continued to push for the acceptance of the charter, visiting individual companies himself to try to persuade them. In the end, strong pressure from environmental NGOs and from the public proved to be the deciding factor. The Global Environmental Charter was officially announced in April 1991, stating that "each company must aim at being a good global corporate citizen, recognizing that grappling with environmental problems is essential to its own existence and its activities."[7]

THE KEIDANREN NATURE CONSERVATION FUND
ESTABLISHMENT OF THE FUND

While announcement of the charter was generally welcomed, some quarters criticized the charter as just a piece of paper that made no commitment to real action. In response, Keidanren decided to establish a fund

7. Keidanren Web site < http://www.keidanren.or.jp > (November 1998).

that would collect money from member corporations and disburse that money to NGOs conducting conservation projects overseas. At the suggestion of Conservation International, a group of Japanese business leaders was sent to Washington, D.C., in 1991 to investigate how professional environmental NGOs in the United States operate and what sort of projects they conduct. Deeply impressed with the sophistication and professionalism of such NGOs as Conservation International and The Nature Conservancy, the members of the mission became convinced that funds provided to such organizations would be used efficiently and effectively.

Following the Washington, D.C., mission, a Committee on Nature Conservation was formed; it became the parent body of the KNCF. Yasuo Goto, chairman and chief executive officer of the Yasuda Fire and Marine Insurance Co., was appointed as the committee's first chairman, and the committee began operations in September 1992. Its creation received much attention, because the committee was viewed as the first sign that the environmentally conscious Hiraiwa had begun to translate the words of the Global Environmental Charter into action. The committee was also partially intended as a means of mitigating heightened trade frictions and improving Japan's relations with the United States and Europe, since it was thought that Japanese business support for the powerful and politically influential environmental NGOs would have a positive impact on economic relations with the United States and Europe. The ultimate motivation behind the establishment of the KNCF was to educate and promote awareness among business leaders by supporting nature conservation activities, and to provide opportunities for corporations to become involved in environmental issues. By supporting NGOs and their projects through the KNCF, it was anticipated that corporations would go on to develop their own projects at a later stage.

STRUCTURE OF THE FUND

Rather than make the KNCF an endowment, it was decided that it would be more meaningful to raise funds annually for use within a given year. Hiraiwa's thinking was that the Keidanren Method should not be used for this purpose, since it emphasized peer pressure from the industries rather than the voluntary gestures of individual corporations; he preferred that voluntary donations be sought from the member corporations and from the personal pockets of business leaders.

It was also decided from the beginning that the KNCF would only support overseas projects. One reason was the urgent need for nature conservation efforts in developing nations, such as preserving the rain forests in Asia, and the strategic importance of support in these areas. A second reason was the perception that Japanese NGOs were already adequately addressing the various conservation issues in Japan, thus making them a lesser priority. In addition, since the KNCF was not familiar with NGOs, it initially focused on support for established overseas NGOs that were known to have extensive experience in the field.

When the KNCF started in 1992, it asked The Nature Conservancy, and especially its director of the Japan Program, Lori Forman, for advice and assistance in reading grant applications and evaluating projects and organizations. Owing to this, in the KNCF's early years The Nature Conservancy, Conservation International, and the World Wildlife Fund received a major portion of the total grants. Gradually, the KNCF began to approach Japanese environmental NGOs as well, and despite initial skepticism those NGOs became increasingly receptive to the Fund's efforts. The KNCF now works with both overseas and domestic NGOs. Even today, however, The Nature Conservancy, Conservation International, and other American and European NGOs still contribute significantly to the Fund's activities by acting as match-makers between the Fund and indigenous NGOs in developing nations.

ORGANIZATION OF THE FUND

The Global Environment Bureau of Keidanren coordinates the work of the Committee on Nature Conservation. The committee, comprised of the chief executive officers of member corporations, meets annually to decide on the basic principles of the KNCF, such as how the Fund will operate, how it should approach companies, and which projects should receive priority. The committee is in charge of all aspects of the KNCF and is currently chaired by Hirotaro Higuchi, honorary chairman of Asahi Breweries, Ltd., who succeeded Goto in July 1998. Once the committee has reached its decisions, the KNCF Secretariat is responsible for raising the necessary funds. The Secretariat is in regular contact with the NGOs throughout the application process. It accepts applications, screens them, and answers questions from the NGOs.

The KNCF accepts donations from Japanese corporations, individuals, and trade associations, as well as from foreign companies with operations in Japan. Total donations add up to roughly ¥200 million (US$1.7 million) yearly, and nearly all of that amount is used to support various nature conservation projects. The administrative costs of the KNCF

Secretariat are covered separately, through annual membership fees charged for the Committee on Nature Conservation. Approximately 150 corporations belong to the committee, and the fees total roughly ¥60 million (US$518,000) yearly.

In addition to regular donations, the KNCF accepts several other types of donations, including donations of equipment, such as computers, cars, bulldozers, and other machinery; "*tsumori* (intended)" donations, whereby a corporation or individual makes a financial contribution to the Fund on behalf of another person as a form of gift or award; and KNCF credit cards, where a certain percentage of monthly charges on the credit card is donated to the Fund by the credit card companies.

GRANT MAKING

Grant applications to the Fund are first screened by the KNCF Secretariat. A preliminary list of potential donees is drawn up and presented to the Selection Committee for its final selection and approval. The members of the Selection Committee are appointed by the chairman of the Committee on Nature Conservation and include scholars and journalists who are experts in the field of nature conservation.

Because the KNCF is limited in its capacity to visit NGOs or actual project sites, the screening process is restricted to applicants who initiate contact with the Fund. The inability for on-site inspection means that funds are normally disbursed to NGOs with which the KNCF is familiar or to well-established NGOs with good reputations. The Fund occasionally asks grant-making NGOs and other related organizations, such as the John D. and Katherine T. MacArthur Foundation, to provide references for indigenous NGOs in developing countries. Some recent grants made by the KNCF included funding for the production of organic foods on degraded slope lands in southern China; for a fishing reform project in Indonesia; for biodiversity conservation in Tibet; for a conservation education program in Bhutan; and for a project to rescue and maintain mangrove forests in the Philippines.

For domestic NGOs, in addition to screening the application itself, the KNCF also occasionally interviews the organization's staff to find out more about the proposed project. Because the number of Japanese NGOs capable of carrying out overseas conservation projects is small, the KNCF does tend to support a set group. The Japan International Volunteer Center, for example, has received grants for sustainable forestry projects in Cambodia and Laos; the Wild Bird Society of Japan has received grants to study important biological areas in Southeast Asia using wild birds as a measure of biodiversity; Friends of the Earth Japan has received funding to identify biodiversity hot spots in the Russian Far East; and the Common Agenda Roundtable has received a grant to support Indonesian NGOs.

The Fund tries to maintain an even balance between domestic and overseas NGOs in grant making, but doing so has been difficult given that Japanese environmental NGOs are still in the early stages of development in terms of organizational strength, outreach, expertise, and professionalism. Therefore, although the KNCF would like to increase the proportion of grants to domestic NGOs, in reality 50 percent is the maximum percentage that the Fund can allocate to them. Particularly given that KNCF donations are collected on an annual basis, there is a need to fund NGOs and projects that will have a fairly quick demonstrable impact.

FUTURE DIRECTION OF AND CHALLENGES FOR THE KNCF

THE FUND'S ACHIEVEMENTS

The KNCF was established as a result of a confluence of global and domestic trends. Strident demands from the NGO sector and the general public for the business community to take serious action to protect the environment, better corporate understanding of environmental issues, growing pressure on the overseas operations of Japanese corporations to be responsible corporate citizens, and the leadership of a new Keidanren chairman who believed in the "coexistence" of business and the environment—all these combined to provide a powerful incentive for the creation of this new mechanism for environmental philanthropy.

To date, the KNCF has successfully served as an intermediary organization between Japanese corporations interested in funding overseas environmental projects and environmental NGOs seeking corporate funding. In particular, the KNCF mechanism has proven to be an ideal vehicle for companies that prefer to take a hands-off approach to supporting environmental NGOs or nature conservation projects. Although there are some Japanese companies that have chosen to set up their own funds to support nature conservation projects within and outside of Japan, generally speaking most companies believe that all the company has to do is donate money to the KNCF and the Fund will take care of the rest. In this way, corporations are not only relieved of the work but are also able to support projects they could not otherwise have known about. The intermediary function of the KNCF also implies less risk for the corporations, because it reduces the possibility of wasted time and funds.

The KNCF has also served to educate corporations and corporate executives and to increase their awareness of environmental issues. In some instances, the Fund has even encouraged corporations to become involved in environmental projects. One successful example of increased corporate awareness is Sekisui Kagaku, a large chemical company and a regular contributor to the Fund. The company recently committed an annual general contribution of ¥50 million (US$432,000) for three years as part of the company's 50th anniversary commemoration. Although this generous contribution demonstrates that Sekisui Kagaku is serious about the environment, for undisclosed reasons the company does not want its name publicized, thus making the KNCF mechanism an ideal choice. Sekisui has also become active in addressing domestic environmental issues. The company works with the Wild Bird Society of Japan, and its employees participate as volunteers in various projects conducted by the NGO.

The KNCF moreover has proven successful in enhancing the positive image of Keidanren, especially outside of Japan where environmental issues are much more actively debated. This reflects positively on the companies that have donated to the Fund.

FUTURE CHALLENGES

Despite the positive impact it has had to date, the KNCF is faced with serious questions regarding its future direction. Should it remain an intermediary body, collecting funds and disbursing them to NGOs, or does it want to become more active in other areas? How can the KNCF expand its capacity and skills in identifying NGOs and selecting projects?

The KNCF currently has a staff of five individuals who are seconded from various corporations and leave after a two- to three-year tenure. This system of rotation prevents the development of a monopoly of power or a bias toward certain organizations. It also permits seconded staff to gain valuable experience that can be applied once they return to their original corporations. The negative side of this system is that seconded staff often leave just as they start to become familiar with environmental issues, the NGOs, their activities, and the people that they work with. The new staff have to start all over again and repeat the same learning process, which can be confusing and frustrating for the NGOs. Finding a solution that balances these pros and cons is another challenge for the future.

As noted earlier, the chairmanship of the Committee on Nature Conservation has just passed from Yasuo Goto to Hirotaro Higuchi. Whether this will lead to major changes in the structure or focus of the KNCF is yet to be seen, but Higuchi's interest in supporting domestic environmental projects in addition to overseas projects will undoubtedly have repercussions.

A more fundamental question, however, is whether Keidanren is committed to maintaining the KNCF. Given the positive reception that the KNCF has enjoyed from the media, the general public, and the NGO community, it would be a shame not to keep up the momentum. It would be especially meaningful if Keidanren and the individual companies involved refused to quit now, in a time of great economic difficulties. Such a commitment would send a strong signal that corporate activities are not just about making money but are also about making contributions to the local community and to the global environment.

About the Contributors

TADASHI YAMAMOTO is President of the Japan Center for International Exchange (JCIE), which he founded in 1970. Mr. Yamamoto is currently a member as well as the Japanese director of the Trilateral Commission, the UK-Japan 2000 Group, the Japanese-German Dialogue Forum, and the Korea-Japan Forum, and a member of the Korea-Japan Joint Committee for Promoting History Studies. He also serves as a member of the boards of the Asian Community Trust and the Japan NPO Center. He was appointed a member of the Prime Minister's Commission on "Japan's Goals in the 21st Century" in March 1999. Mr. Yamamoto is editor/author of books on civil society and the nonprofit sector, including *Emerging Civil Society in the Asia Pacific Community* (1995), *The Nonprofit Sector in Japan* (1998), and *Deciding the Public Good* (1999).

KIMBERLY GOULD ASHIZAWA is a freelance consultant and editor. She assisted in establishing the U.S. operations of the Japan Foundation Center for Global Partnership, serving as program officer for the intellectual exchange grant-making program and overseeing the Center's publications from 1991 to 1999. Previously, she worked as a research assistant for the U.S.-Japan Management Studies Center of the Wharton School of Business, as well as for several high-tech and media firms in the United States and Japan. Ms. Ashizawa received a B.A. in international relations from the University of Pennsylvania and an M.A. in East Asian studies from Columbia University.

ANUCHAT POUNGSOMLEE is Associate Professor in the Faculty of Environment and Resource Studies, Mahidol University at Salaya, Thailand. Dr. Anuchat also serves as secretary-general of Civicnet Institute, a networking organization among various civic groups throughout Thailand. The Institute plays an important role in promoting civil society in the areas of training, networking, and publishing. Through Civicnet and Mahidol University, Dr. Anuchat conducts various research and training programs. His current research project reviews the state of knowledge about civil society in Thailand. *Thai Civil Society: The Making of Thai Citizens* (1999) is his newest publication.

EKA BUDIANTA is an Indonesian poet and environmentalist. He graduated from the Leadership for Environment and Development Program after conducting field studies in Costa Rica (1995); Okinawa, Japan (1996); and Zimbabwe (1997). Mr. Budianta has published several books on tourism, education, and the environment. In 1986, Mr. Budianta received the Ashoka Award as a public innovator. He served as the executive director of the Friends of the Environment Fund in Jakarta from 1994 until 1998. He is currently executive director of Friends of Aqua Foundation and director of social affairs for PT Tirta Investama.

SUSAN HUBBARD, Program Officer and Research Associate for the Japan Center for International Exchange from 1994 to 1997, is Program Associate in the Intellectual Exchange Program of the Japan Foundation Center for Global Partnership. Ms. Hubbard was the 1993–1994 Brian Kane Fellow at the Kiyosato Educational Experiment Project in Kiyosato, Japan. She received a B.A. in political science and Asian studies from Northwestern University and an M.I.A. in economic and political development from Columbia University's School of International and Public Affairs.

HIROSHI PETER KAMURA is Executive Director of the Japan Center for International Exchange, Inc. (U.S.A.) in New York, as well as the U.S. representative of JCIE/Japan, Tokyo. A graduate of Sophia University in Tokyo, he received his M.A. in international relations from Georgetown University in Washington, D.C., as a Fulbright scholar. Mr. Kamura is the author of the Japan section of the Rockefeller Foundation's *International Relations Research: Emerging Trends Outside the United States 1981– 1983*; *The Role of Private Institutions in International Relations: Lessons from Trans-Atlantic Relations and Challenges for Japan* (1991); and "The

Role of U.S. Foundations in the Asia Pacific: A Historical Perspective," in *Emerging Civil Society in the Asia Pacific Regional Community* (1995).

HIDEKO KATSUMATA is Executive Secretary of the Japan Center for International Exchange (JCIE). A graduate of the University of the Sacred Heart, she joined the Japan Council of International Understanding (which was reorganized as JCIE in 1970) in 1969. She has been executive secretary since 1985 and is responsible for overall office management as well as managing major conferences JCIE sponsors. She serves as Planning Committee member of the Japan NPO Center, Steering Committee member of the Tokyo Voluntary Action Center, and Screening Committee member of the Tokyo International Exchange Foundation. Her recent publications include "Corporate Philanthropy in Thailand" (*IRI Angle*, 1995), "U.S.-Japan Women's Dialogue: Women Talk to Women" (*Gaiko Forum*, 1995), and *International Program Officers* (1997).

MIO KAWASHIMA is Program Officer of the Japan Center for International Exchange (JCIE). Her responsibilities since joining JCIE in 1996 include writing the *Civil Society Monitor* newsletter and coordinating the China-Japan-U.S. Research and Dialogue Project. Previously she worked for SBC Warburg Japan Ltd. as an equity analyst from 1994 to 1996. Ms. Kawashima received a B.A. in economics from Keio University and an M.A. in international economics and finance from Brandeis University.

PAIBOON WATTANASIRITHAM is Director-General of the Government Savings Bank, Chairman of the Thailand Rural Reconstruction Movement, and a committee member of the Asia Pacific Philanthropy Consortium. Prior to working in the field of social development, he worked for the Bank of Thailand for 14 years, served as the president of the Stock Exchange of Thailand from 1980 to 1982, and was senior vice president of the Thai Danu Bank Company Limited from 1983 to 1988. Mr. Paiboon is involved in several nongovernmental and governmental organizations.

CRISTINA V. PAVIA is Casebank Development Coordinator for the training and consulting unit of Philippine Business for Social Progress (PBSP). Ms. Pavia previously served as senior executive assistant supporting the executive director in the handling of board and executive committee office affairs and in organizing institutional program and operations review for the management team. Ms. Pavia joined PBSP in 1988 as program officer assigned to develop, monitor, and evaluate programs in rice-producing Central Luzon provinces. She also handled membership involvement relations in the PBSP Cebu Office, including helping to initiate the Cebu Hillyland Development Program in 1988. Ms. Pavia earned a Certificate in Fundraising and Promotion for Non-Profits at the New York University Center for Continuing Education in 1991.

NGUYEN VAN THANH was Executive Vice President of the Vietnam Union of Friendship Organizations until he retired in January 1999. Mr. Thanh was responsible for operational issues involving aid to Vietnam from foreign nongovernmental organizations (NGOs). He played an integral part in increasing Vietnamese understanding of the role of foreign NGOs and philanthropy.

ZHANG YE is Director of the China Program at the Asia Foundation and a researcher at the Chinese Academy of Social Sciences. Prior to working for the Asia Foundation, she served as assistant to the representative of the Ford Foundation China Office. Zhang received her M.P.A. from Harvard University's Kennedy School of Government and received a diploma in American Studies from Smith College in the United States. She has published several articles concerning the development of the Chinese nongovernmental and nonprofit sector. She co-authored the China report for *Philanthropy and Law in Asia* and contributed articles on Chinese non-government organizations and foundations to the book *Emerging Civil Society in the Asia Pacific Community* (1995).

Japan Center for
International Exchange

Founded in 1970, the Japan Center for International Exchange (JCIE) is an independent, nonprofit, and nonpartisan organization dedicated to strengthening Japan's role in international affairs. JCIE believes that Japan faces a major challenge in augmenting its positive contributions to the international community, in keeping with its position as one of the world's largest industrial democracies. Operating in a country where policy making has traditionally been dominated by the government bureaucracy, JCIE has played an important role in broadening debate on Japan's international responsibilities by conducting international and cross-sectional programs of exchange, research, and discussion.

JCIE creates opportunities for informed policy discussions; it does not take policy positions. JCIE programs are carried out with the collaboration and cosponsorship of many organizations. The contacts developed through these working relationships are crucial to JCIE's efforts to increase the number of Japanese from the private sector engaged in meaningful policy research and dialogue with overseas counterparts. JCIE receives no government subsidies; rather, funding comes from private foundation grants, corporate contributions, and contracts.